Homer's *Odyssey*
A Reading Guide

T0333146

Henry Power

Edinburgh University Press

© Henry Power, 2011

Edinburgh University Press Ltd
22 George Square, Edinburgh

www.euppublishing.com

Typeset in 10.5/13 Sabon
by Servis Filmsetting Ltd, Stockport, Cheshire, and
printed and bound in Great Britain by
CPI Antony Rowe, Chippenham and Eastbourne

A CIP record for this book is available from the British Library

ISBN 978 0 7486 4110 9 (hardback)
ISBN 978 0 7486 4109 3 (paperback)

The right of Henry Power
to be identified as author of this work
has been asserted in accordance with
the Copyright, Designs and Patents Act 1988.

Contents

Acknowledgements

This book has benefited hugely from the Oxford commentary on the *Odyssey*, by A. Heubeck and others (1988–92). I have also learned a great deal from Peter Jones's 1988 commentary on Lattimore's version – highly recommended to English readers who want to study the complete poem in translation. The other books which have been particularly useful are Irene de Jong's *A Narratological Comentary on Homer's Odyssey* (2001) and Edith Hall's excellent *The Return of Ulysses* (2008). I would like to thank Sally Bushell, the editor of the series, for her help and encouragement – and Jackie Jones at Edinburgh University Press for guiding the book firmly and efficiently towards publication. Llewelyn Morgan introduced me to the *Odyssey* in the first place, and kindly read an early draft of this book, saving me from several embarrassments (surviving errors are my own, of course). Sophie Humes has been more helpful than I can say.

pp. 23–35 (Book I), 37–46 (Book VI), 50–66 (Book IX), 69–80 (Book XIII), 83–93 (Book XXIII) from *The Odyssey of Homer*, Translated and with an Introduction by Richmond Lattimore, © 1965, 1967 by Richmond Lattimore; © Renewed 1995 by Alice B. Lattimore. Reprinted by permission of HarperCollins Publishers.

Note on the text

The text is taken from Richmond Lattimore, trans., *The Odyssey of Homer* (New York: Harper, 1965), which has been chosen for its closeness to the original, and which is reprinted by permission of HarperCollins Publishers. All line references are to Lattimore's translation, and not the original Greek, though the two often coincide. Quotations from the *Iliad* are also from Lattimore's version (Chicago: University of Chicago Press, 1951). References to 'Graves' are to Robert Graves, *The Greek Myths*, 2 vols, 2nd edn (Harmondsworth: Penguin, 1960), and are to section rather than page number.

Series Preface

The form of the long poem has been of fundamental importance to Literary Studies from the time of Homer onwards. The Reading Guides to Long Poems Series seeks to celebrate and explore this form in all its diversity across a range of authors and periods. Major poetic works – *The Odyssey, The Faerie Queene, Paradise Lost, The Prelude, In Memoriam, The Waste Land* – emerge as defining expressions of the culture which produced them. One of the main aims of the series is to make contemporary readers aware of the importance of the long poem for our literary and national heritage.

How 'long' is a long poem? In 'The Philosophy of Composition' Edgar Allan Poe asserted that there is 'a distinct limit, as regards length, to all works of literary art – the limit of a single sitting'. Defined against this, a long poem must be one which *exceeds* the limit of a single sitting, requiring sustained attention over a considerable period of time for its full appreciation. However, the concept of poetic length is not simply concerned with the number of lines in a poem, or the time it takes to read it. In 'From Poe to Valéry' T. S. Eliot defends poetic length on the grounds that 'it is only in a poem of some length that a variety of moods can be expressed . . . These parts can form a whole more than the sum of the parts; a whole such that the pleasure we derive from the reading of any part is enhanced by our grasp of the whole.' Along with Eliot, the Series Editors believe that poetic length creates a unique space for a varied play of meaning and tone, action and reflection, that results in particular kinds of reading and interpretation not possible for shorter works. The Reading Guides are therefore concerned with communicating the pleasure and enjoyment of engaging with the form in a range of ways – focusing on particular episodes, tracing out patterns of poetic imagery, exploring form, reading and re-reading the text – in order to allow the reader to experience the multiple interpretative layers that the long poem holds within it. We also believe that a self-awareness about *how* we read the long poem may help to provide the modern reader with a necessary fresh perspective upon the genre.

The Reading Guides to Long Poems Series will engage with major works in new and innovative ways in order to revitalise the form of the long poem for a new generation. The series will present shorter 'long poems' in their entirety, while the longest are represented by a careful selection of essential parts. Long poems have often been read aloud, imitated, or even translated in excerpts, so there is good precedent for appreciating them through selective reading. Nevertheless, it is to be hoped that readers will use the Guides alongside an appreciation of the work in its entirety or, if they have not previously done so, go on to read the whole poem.

Ultimately the Reading Guides to Long Poems Series seeks to be of lasting value to the discipline of Literary Studies by revitalising a form which is in danger of being marginalised by the current curriculum but is central to our understanding of our own literature, history and culture.

Sally Bushell with Isobel Armstrong and Colin Burrow

Chapter 1

Mapping and Making

The *Odyssey* as an Epic Poem

An epic is a long poem. It usually focuses on the exploits of a single hero. It is usually characterised by an elevated or archaic tone ('epic diction'), its author drawing on a vocabulary not used in everyday speech: we are more likely to encounter a 'steed' or 'charger' in an epic poem, than to meet a horse. It usually describes the activities of gods, and their involvement in human affairs. Its subject matter usually has some claim to universal – or at least national – significance, rather than being concerned simply with the particular actions of particular people. To read an epic is not simply to immerse oneself in the lives of others; it is to receive a cultural education. The best known example in English is John Milton's *Paradise Lost*.

Very few of these rules are obeyed by all epic poets; only length could be reasonably described as a universal quality. Most of them are based on people's readings of two poems attributed to 'Homer': the *Iliad* and the *Odyssey*. These are the two earliest surviving works of European literature. Little is known for certain about their composition, but we can assume that the poems were intended for oral performance. The *Odyssey* contains some descriptions of bards singing narrative songs, and these may give us some idea of how the poem was originally performed (see in particular I.325–44; VIII.62–95). We have almost no information about Homer – and cannot even be certain that these two poems were composed by the same person. Indeed, some critics have argued that neither poem should properly be regarded as the work of a single poet; we might instead see it as the product of an oral tradition, passed down from generation to generation, augmented and improved by any number of poets (see pp. 95–8 below for more details). We can assume that Homer spoke Greek, but it is hard to say where in the

Greek-speaking world he might have lived; by the fifth century BC (when his place in the canon was assured), seven cities were putting themselves forward as his birthplace.

It is especially hard to come up with a date for the poem. Its composition may not even have been confined to a single generation. It seems probable, though, that the *Odyssey* came to be written down towards the end of the eighth century BC – and that its transcription was the result of the arrival of the alphabet in Greece. But there is a gap of at least a century between the date usually now given to the *Odyssey* (*c*.700 BC, around 30 years after the *Iliad*) and the moment when references to the Homeric poems start appearing. From the sixth century (and perhaps earlier) the poems were performed in public by rhapsodes – professional performers of Homeric verse. They recited from memory, but did not improvise: the text had become fixed.

Homeric epic has some striking stylistic features, which can be off-putting to a first-time reader. Its style is characterised, above all, by repetition. There are repetitions of single words, such as the epithets used to describe the various characters. There are repetitions of whole lines, such as those used to indicate the time of day ('But when the young Dawn showed again with her rosy fingers'). Groups of verses recur; we sometimes find that an account of (say) a feast reappears verbatim a few books later. In all, about 1,000 of the *Odyssey*'s lines are repeated at some point, out of a total of around 12,000. And there are repeated situations which – though rendered differently – conform to an identifiable type. These repetitions give a distinctive flavour to epic poetry, highlighting connections between different parts of the poem. Most critics would now attribute them to the poem's origins in oral composition (see under Contexts below), but they have nonetheless been imitated by later epic poets who worked solely with ink and paper.

The same can be said of the similes, which are perhaps the most distinctive feature of Homeric (and epic) style – much imitated and parodied by later authors. The poet regularly interrupts his narrative in order to develop an elaborate point of comparison for the thing he is describing. These similes are at times so extended that they constitute miniature narratives, embedded in the central one. To give one example, when the shipwrecked Odysseus catches sight of land, Homer gives a sketch of his hero's emotions:

> And as welcome as the show of life again in a father
> is to his children, when he has lain sick, suffering strong pains,
> and wasting long away, and the hateful death spirit has brushed him,
> but then, and it is welcome, the gods set him free of his sickness,

so welcome appeared land and forest now to Odysseus,
and he swam . . . (V.394–9)

As will be seen from this example, the function of these similes is not
simply to clarify the nature of the situation being described (and often
their effect is to complicate). The simile quoted above tells us that the
sight of land is welcome to Odysseus, but it does so in a strange way,
comparing the land to the dying father although it is Odysseus who has
been at the point of death. And it anticipates the end of the poem, when
we will see a father – Odysseus – returning to his son, as if from the
dead. Like many Homeric similes, it deepens our understanding of the
atmosphere and emotions surrounding a particular event – without necessarily enhancing our ability to picture it. Similes also offer us (and this
is more regularly the case in the *Odyssey* than in the *Iliad*) a fascinating
glimpse into the world of the poet and his audience.

The *Odyssey* and the *Iliad*

The adventures recounted in the *Odyssey* take place in the aftermath
of the Trojan War – which also provides the backdrop to Homer's
Iliad (the poem's title is taken from Ilion, another name for Troy).
Specifically, the *Iliad* (set during the ninth and penultimate year of the
siege of Troy) deals with the anger of Achilles, the greatest of the Greek
warriors. He has been insulted by Agamemnon, the leader of the Greek
expedition, and refuses to fight. As a result, the Greeks suffer terrible
losses – but it is only when Achilles' greatest friend Patroklos is killed by
the Trojan prince Hektor that he returns to battle. He kills Hektor and
attempts to desecrate his corpse, dragging it behind his chariot. Hektor's
father, Priam, begs Achilles for the return of his son's body. Achilles
eventually relents after Hektor's father goes in person to Achilles to beg
for his body's return, and the poem ends with Hector's funeral. Very
few of the most celebrated episodes in the story of the Trojan war – the
elopement of Helen with Paris, the death of Achilles (through an arrow
in his heel), the wooden horse – are covered by the plot of the *Iliad*. It is
an intensive study of a particular situation, which unfolds over a period
of days.

The *Odyssey* is very different in subject matter, in tone, and in construction. Whereas the subject matter of the *Iliad* is martial prowess,
and the bloody struggles between groups of great warriors, the *Odyssey*
focuses far more on the domestic lives of its characters – Odysseus above
all. The *Odyssey*'s characters are more diverse; we hear about princesses,

witches, monsters, beggars, nymphs and swineherds – whereas the *Iliad* is focused only on those who fight at Troy, and their appendages. This affects the tone which – while still necessarily adhering to the conventions of epic poetry – is more down-to-earth (see pp. 17–19 below). In terms of construction, the *Iliad* is straightforward; the plot advances chronologically. The *Odyssey*, in contrast, is deliberately and engagingly complicated. The hero's entrance is delayed for four books, and we only hear of his many adventures in a piece of retrospective narration. It is another striking difference that a substantial proportion of the *Odyssey* is narrated in the first person.

In antiquity, it was almost universally believed that the *Iliad* and the *Odyssey* were the work of the same poet. There was, however, a small group – the 'Khorizontes' or 'Separatists' – who held that the *Odyssey* must be by a different poet, largely on the basis of its less obviously heroic subject matter. Opinion on the topic is now divided, and it is hard to imagine the emergence of hard evidence capable of proving the point one way or the other. It is beyond reasonable doubt that whoever composed the *Odyssey*, assuming we can talk in terms of a single 'composer' (see pp. 94–8 below), knew the *Iliad* well. Besides some particular apparent references and adaptations, and the fact that the *Odyssey* fills gaps left by the *Iliad*, the influence of the earlier poem can be felt throughout. The question remains: is the *Odyssey* the work of the same poet, modifying, refining and completing his earlier work – or is it by a later poet, writing in the shadow of the *Iliad*-poet, but nonetheless attempting something different in character? One famous view is that of the first-century AD critic Longinus, who wrote that Homer:

> made the whole body of the *Iliad*, which was written at the height of his powers, dramatic and exciting, whereas most of the *Odyssey* consists of narrative, which is a characteristic of old age. Homer in the *Odyssey* may be compared to the setting sun: the size remains without the force. (Longinus 1965: 13)

The Metre

Greek metre works differently from English metre. In English verse, attention is paid to whether a particular syllable is stressed or unstressed. In Greek verse, the crucial issue is whether a syllable is 'long' or 'short' (though some readers prefer the terms 'heavy' or 'light'). The *Odyssey*, like the *Iliad*, is written in dactylic hexameters. A hexameter is a line of verse with six metrical 'feet'. Each of the first four feet can be filled either by a dactyl (a long syllable followed by two short syllables: – ˘ ˘) or a spondee (two long syllables: – –). The fifth foot is almost always a dactyl, and the sixth foot always effectively a spondee (even if the final syllable is short, the pause at the end of the line makes it sound as long), meaning that each line ends with a distinctive cadence. The length of a line thus varies between thirteen and seventeen syllables. The first verse of the *Odyssey* is a good example of a heavily dactylic line:

— ˘ ˘ |— ˘ ˘|—— ˘ ˘|— ˘ ˘ |—— ˘ ˘|— —

andra moi ennepe Mousa polutrōpon hos mala polla

Tell me, Muse, of the man of many ways, who was driven

while the third verse is more heavily spondaic

— —|—— —|— ˘ ˘ |— ˘˘|— ˘ ˘|— —

pollōn d' anthrōpōn iden astea kai noon egnō

Many were they whose cities he saw, whose minds he learned of

The quantitative hexameter is a difficult thing to represent in English verse. Samuel Taylor Coleridge made a spirited attempt to reproduce the sound of the Homeric hexameter – and, in the process, to describe its effect on the listener:

—— ˘ ˘ |—— ˘ ˘ | — —|—— ˘ ˘ |- ˘ ˘ |- —

Strongly it bears us along in swelling and limitless billows,

— ˘ ˘| — —|— ˘ ˘|— ˘ ˘|— ˘ ˘ | — —

Nothing before and nothing behind but the sky and the ocean.

There have been attempts (most notably by Matthew Arnold in the 1860s) to translate the Homeric epics into quantitative English verse – but these attempts have not found favour with readers. A lot of energy has gone into finding an English verse form which might correspond to the Greek hexameter; this is discussed in detail in pp. 103–17 below. The translation used for this commentary, that of Richmond Lattimore (1965), gestures towards Homeric metre by containing six stresses per line. It is, however, much looser than Homeric verse, and some readers have complained that it reads like prose.

Setting

The focus of the *Odyssey* is the island of Ithaka. This probably corresponds to the island now known as Ithaki, though there are some difficulties with this identification; the details Homer gives of the island group at IX.21–7 cannot be made to tally exactly with the geography of the Ionian islands (though many have attempted to do so, see Bradford 1963; Bittleston, Diggle and Underhill 2005). And if it is difficult to identify Ithaka, it is trickier still to say where the Phaiakians, or the Cyclops, or Kalypso live. Odysseus' travels take place largely in the realm of fantasy, and we can reasonably regard Ithaka as being part of that fictional world. Most scholars place Homer in the eastern Aegean, or even in what is now Turkey; his representation of the westernmost points of Greek civilisation inevitably draws on hearsay and poetic invention, rather than firsthand geographical knowledge.

Summary

In the *Odyssey*, we hear of events that occur within a ten-year period, but this is largely through reminiscence and retrospective narration. The poem's plot unfolds over the course of forty-one days. Its structure can only be fully appreciated by a reading of the entire poem (this is perhaps the single strongest argument against those who believe it to be an amalgam of various shorter poems; see under Contexts below). There is a great deal of pleasure to be had from reading excerpts, but this pleasure is enhanced by an understanding of where they fall in the scheme of the poem as a whole. The *Odyssey* can be divided into three clear sections: Books I–IV (the '*Telemacheia*'), in which we see Telemachos beginning to assert himself in Ithaka, and seeking news of his father abroad; Books V–XII, in which we hear of Odysseus' adventures as he tries to reach Ithaka; and Books XIII–XXIV, in which Odysseus re-establishes himself in Ithaka, and avenges himself against the suitors.

When the *Odyssey* opens, Odysseus is with Kalypso on Ogygia. His household in Ithaka has been overrun by suitors, who are demanding that Penelope, Odysseus' wife, marry one of them. Twenty years have passed since he left Ithaka for Troy. A summary of the whole poem is given here. Sections reproduced in this edition are highlighted in italics.

Book I   The poet appeals to the Muse, and asks her to sing of Odysseus' return: the narrative will begin after all the other Greek warriors have returned home from Troy. It opens on Olympus, where the gods are discussing the death of the Mykenian king, Agamemnon, murdered on his return from Troy. Athene appeals to Zeus to allow Odysseus to return safely to Ithaka; Zeus consents. Athene then travels to Ithaka, disguised as Mentes, where she finds a number of suitors dominating the household – all seeking to marry Odysseus' wife, Penelope. Telemachos entertains Athene, and she urges him to call a public assembly, and then to seek news of his father, from Nestor in Pylos and Menelaos in Sparta.

Book II Telemachos calls a public assembly, at which he criticises the suitors' behaviour. The suitors are indignant, blame Penelope, and demand that Telemachos begin arrangements for his mother's marriage. An omen appears in the sky, but the suitors ignore it. Telemachos makes arrangements for his trip to Pylos and Sparta. Athene, having assumed the identity of Mentor (an old friend of Odysseus), has prepared a ship, and now travels with Telamachos

Book III Telemachos and Athene/Mentor arrive in Pylos, where they are welcomed by Nestor and his sons. Nestor, the oldest of the Greeks to have fought at Troy, tells them about the various homecomings of other warriors – most notably Agamemnon. He has heard nothing about Odysseus in the past ten years, but suggests that Telemachos goes to Sparta, and asks Menelaos. Athene disappears, and Telemachos travels on, with Nestor's son, Pisistratos.

Book IV Telemachos and Pisistratos arrive in Sparta, and are welcomed by Menelaos, who is once again living with his wife Helen (whose elopement with Paris had sparked the Trojan War). Menelaos tells of his own difficult journey home from Troy, and of how he was marooned on an island near Egypt. Here Proteus, the Old Man of the Sea, told him (amongst other things) that Odysseus was being detained by the nymph Kalypso, on the island of Ogygia. The suitors find out about Telemachos' journey, and decide to ambush and kill him on his return. Penelope also finds out about her son's disappearance. She is upset, but Athene (in the form of Penelope's sister, Ipthime) comforts her in a dream.

Book V On Olympos, Athene complains about Kalypso's imprisonment of Odysseus. Hermes, the messenger of the gods, is sent to Ogygia, to tell Kalypso that she must let him go. Kalypso offers Odysseus immortality if he will stay with her, but he refuses, and they eat one last meal together – he eating ordinary food, she eating ambrosia, the food of the gods. Odysseus builds himself a raft, and sets sail. After seventeen days, Poseidon sees him, and unleashes a terrible storm, which destroys the raft (Poseidon holds a grudge against Odysseus; see Book IX). Odysseus narrowly escapes death, and is washed up, naked, on the coast of Phaiakia.

Book VI Athene appears in a dream to Nausikaa, a Phaiakian princess, and suggests that she goes down to the shore to wash some clothes. Here she encounters the shipwrecked Odysseus, naked and bedraggled. He throws himself at her mercy, and she accepts his supplication.

Having fed and clothed him, she tells him to go to the city and find her parents, King Alkinoös and Queen Arete.

Book VII   Athene, in the form of a young woman, shows Odysseus the way to the royal palace. Here he asks Arete and Alkinoös for help. They welcome him, and he tells them a version of his story – though he does not yet reveal his name.

Book VIII   The Phaiakians decide that they will take Odysseus back to Ithaka. They celebrate with a banquet, at which the blind poet Demodokos sings about Odysseus' exploits in the Trojan War. This makes Odysseus weep. There are then a series of sporting contests, in which Odysseus only takes part after being aggressively challenged by a Phaiakian nobleman. He amazes the Phaiakians with his skill at the discus. They all return to the banquet, where Demodokos sings about the love affair between the gods Ares and Aphrodite. Odysseus asks him to sing about the Wooden Horse. When he does so, Odysseus weeps again. Alkinoös asks him to reveal his true identity.

Book IX   *In response to Alkinoös, Odysseus tells the Phaiakians his name, and tells them the story of his adventures since leaving Troy, ten years earlier. First, he raided the Kikonians in Thrace. Then, blown off course, he and his men visited the land of the Lotus-eaters. After that, they came to the island of the Cyclopes, where Odysseus' curiosity caused him to take some of his men to the Cyclops Polyphemos' cave. Polyphemos ate six of the men, and Odysseus and a handful of survivors escaped through the hero's cunning: he made Polyphemos drunk, blinded him, and then escaped from the cave by clinging to the underbellies of sheep. Polyphemos cursed Odysseus, and called on his father Poseidon to avenge him.*

Book X   Odysseus continues his narration. He and his men came to the island of the god Aiolos, who gave Odysseus a leather bag containing all of winds except for the westerly wind, which he needed for his journey home. Odysseus' men opened it while he was asleep, and they were driven back to Aiolos, who refused to give them any more help. They then arrived in the land of the Laistrygones, man-eating giants, who destroyed eleven of their twelve ships. The one remaining ship proceeded to the island of the enchantress Circe, who turned several of the men into pigs. Odysseus was able (with the help of Hermes) to overcome her, and persuade her to return his men to human form. Odysseus and Circe lived as lovers for a year, and he then left. Circe told him that, before returning home, he must visit the underworld and consult the prophet Teiresias.

Book XI   Odysseus continues his narration. He and his men arrived in the land of the Kimmerians, and performed the necessary rituals in order to call up the dead. Teiresias gave Odysseus advice, and told him of his future. He met the ghost of his mother Antikleia, of Agamemnon and of Achilles. He also saw the punishments of various sinners.

Book XII   Odysseus continues his narration. Having returned from the underworld, he was given instructions by Circe on how to find his way home. He and his men sailed past the coast of the Sirens, and in between the sea monster Scylla and the whirlpool Charybdis. They eventually came to the island of Trinacria, where there were herds of cattle sacred to the sun-god Helios. Odysseus' men killed and ate these cattle. Helios complained to Zeus, who struck Odysseus' one remaining ship with a thunderbolt. Everyone died in the shipwreck, except for Odysseus himself, who clung to the mast and made it to Ogygia, Kalypso's island.

Book XIII   *After his tale is concluded, the Phaiakians carry the sleeping Odysseus back to Ithaka, along with a great many presents. On their return to Phaiakia, Poseidon punishes them by turning their ship to stone. When Odysseus wakes up, he does not know where he is, because Athene has covered the island in a mist, and thinks the Phaiakians have tricked him. Athene appears to him, disguised as a shepherd. When Odysseus claims to be a fugitive Cretan, she reveals herself as a goddess. Athene gives Odysseus some advice, and disguises him as a beggar.*

Book XIV   As instructed by Athene, Odysseus goes to see the loyal swineherd, Eumaios, despairs of the king ever returning. Odysseus is received generously. He tells Eumaios that he is from Crete, and says he has heard that Odysseus is in Dodona, and will return shortly.

Book XV   Athene visits Telemachos in Sparta, and tells him to return home. She warns him of the suitors' plan to ambush him, and also advises him to visit Eumaios' hut. Telemachos receives gifts from Menelaos and Helen, and returns to Pylos with Pisistratos. He picks up a fugitive prophet, Theoklymenos, and returns quickly to Ithaka. Meanwhile, Eumaios tells Odysseus his life story: he is the son of the king of Sidon, who was captured by pirates and sold as a slave to Odysseus' father. Telemachos lands on Ithaka, having safely avoided the ambush.

Book XVI   Telemachos goes to Eumaios' hut, where he tells the disguised Odysseus about the situation on Ithaka. Athene appears to Odysseus and tells him to reveal himself to Telemachos; she also removes his disguise. Odysseus does as she suggests, and he and Telemachos then plan their course of action. The suitors discover that Telemachos has landed safely, and are furious. Antinoös wants to murder him, but is dissuaded by Amphinomos. Athene again disguises Odysseus as a beggar. He and Telemachos spend the night at Eumaios' hut.

Book XVII   Telemachos goes to the palace to see Penelope. Odysseus also heads there, with Eumaios. On the way they meet Melanthios, an evil goatherd and a supporter of the suitors, who insults Odysseus. Outside the palace they see Odysseus' dog Argos, lying on a dunghill. Argos recognises his master, and dies immediately. Odysseus begs from the suitors. Antinoös throws a footstool at him. Penelope asks to see the beggar, but Odysseus manages to postpone the encounter.

Book XVIII   An arrogant beggar, Iros, challenges Odysseus. In the ensuing fight, Odysseus knocks him out. Penelope comes in and criticises Telemachos for allowing a beggar to be mistreated. The suitors give Penelope presents and restate their intention of remaining in the house until Penelope remarries. Odysseus is insulted by the disloyal maidservant Melantho. He argues with Eurymachos, who also throws a footstool at him (but misses).

Book XIX   Odysseus and Telemachos remove all the weapons from the hall of the palace. Melantho insults Odysseus again, and is chastised by Penelope, who has come to speak to the beggar. Penelope and Odysseus have a long conversation, but Penelope does not recognise him. He tells her that he is acquainted with Odysseus, and believes him to be on the point of returning to Ithaka. Penelope does not believe him. She tells the old nurse Eurykleia to wash the beggar. Eurykleia notices a scar on the beggar's knee, and realises that he is Odysseus – whose knee was wounded by a boar's tusk when he was a boy; he swears her to secrecy. Penelope says that she will marry the man who can equal her husband's prowess with a bow. The following day, she will ask the suitors to string Odysseus' bow, and to shoot an arrow through the tiny holes in a row of twenty axe-blades.

Book XX   Odysseus is worried and has trouble sleeping, but is consoled by Athene. In the morning, he receives favourable omens. He is joined by the faithful oxherd Philoitios. One of the suitors, Ktesippos, insults Odysseus and throws an oxfoot at him. Athene infects the suitors with uncontrollable laughter. The prophet Theoklymenos predicts a gruesome end for them.

Book XXI   Penelope brings out Odysseus' bow, and explains the test. The suitors, in turn, try and fail to string the bow. Odysseus reveals his identity to Eumaios and Philoitios, and tells them to bar the gates of the palace. Odysseus asks for the bow, but the suitors try to prevent him from trying. Telemachos sends Penelope away, and Eumaios gives

Odysseus the bow. He strings it, and shoots an arrow through the axe-heads.

Book XXII Odysseus throws off his beggar's rags, and shoots Antinoös in the throat. He, Telemachos, Eumaios and Philoitios battle against the suitors. During the battle, Melanthios tries to provide the suitors with more armour, but is prevented. Eventually, all of the suitors are killed. Eurykleia names the maidservants who have been disloyal, and Telemachos hangs them. Melanthios is dismembered and castrated.

Book XXIII *Eurykleia tells Penelope that Odysseus has returned and killed the suitors. Penelope remains unconvinced. Odysseus tells the bard Phemios to play wedding music, so that no-one outside the palace will suspect what has happened – but assume that Penelope has finally chosen a husband. Odysseus and Penelope meet, and he eventually persuades her of his identity, through his knowledge of the bed which he built in their room. They go to bed, and tell each other everything that has happened to them over the past twenty years.*

Book XXIV Hermes conducts the souls of the suitors down to the underworld. They meet Agamemnon and Achilles. Agamemnon describes Achilles' funeral. The suitors complain about Penelope, but Agamemnon praises her faithfulness. Meanwhile, in the land of the living, Odysseus goes to see his father Laertes. He again claims to be someone else, but eventually reveals himself, and shows Laertes his scar. Meanwhile, the suitors' families, led by Antinoös' father Eupeithes, meet and plan revenge. Odysseus kills Eupeithes, but Athene prevents the battle from escalating. The poem concludes open-endedly.

Chapter 2
Four Ways of Approaching the Poem

I

The *Odyssey* is a poem about memory. What principally engages the reader in the first half of the poem is the uncertainty as to whether Odysseus will continue to remember his homeland. His return home (Gk *nostos*) is under constant threat, and not only from the people and monsters who try to kill him; he is tested mentally as well as physically. Eating the fruit of the Lotus plant will cause him to 'forget the way home', the nymph Kalypso actively seeks to supplant Penelope's place in his mind, the Sirens' song threatens to lure him from his ship. In these situations, Odysseus needs to keep a firm grip on his identity. This is never more evident than in the poignant final meal shared by Odysseus and Kalypso; the goddess eats ambrosia (the food of the gods), while Odysseus – having refused the immortality she offers – dines on 'such things that mortal people feed on' (V.197). His return to Ithaka becomes inevitable at the start of Book XIII, as the sun sets on his second day among the Phaiakians. Using an extended simile, Homer describes Odysseus' feelings as he watches that sunset:

> and as a man makes for his dinner, when all day
> long his wine-colored oxen have dragged the compact plow for him
> across the field, and the sun's setting is welcome for bringing
> the time to go to his dinner, and as he goes his knees fail him;
> thus welcome now to Odysseus was the sun going under. (XIII.31–5)

As well as indicating Odysseus' love of home, the simile, with its subject matter apparently drawn from the rugged, agricultural landscape of Ithaka, suggests that his memory of the island is deeply engrained. In the second half of the poem, Odysseus' task is different: he has arrived on

Ithaka, and now needs to reawaken the memories of his family and of his compatriots.

On Ithaka, Penelope has been fostering a memory of her husband, and Telemachos – too young to remember his father – has been gathering reminiscences from those who do. Most significantly, he travels to Sparta, where he meets Menelaos and Helen, and hears their memories of Odysseus. As they speak about the recent past, everyone at the banquet begins to weep. Eventually Helen drugs the wine of all those present with 'a medicine / of heartsease, free of gall, to make one forget all sorrows' (IV.120–1; see Bergren 1981). It is a bizarre moment, which reminds us of the pain involved in remembering. Penelope's 'unforgettable sorrow' (I.340), and Odysseus' grief at the Phaiakian banquet are both tied to acts of remembrance. The *Odyssey* is a nostalgic poem, in the word's original sense – from the Greek *nostos* (return) and *algia* (pain).

These acts of remembrance are also both prompted by poetic performances, and it is not mere coincidence that the *Odyssey*, which focuses to such an extent on the memory of people and events, emerged from a tradition of oral poetry founded in memory. Throughout the poem, we are shown a culture in which people share memories with others. This happens informally: we hear recollections of Odysseus from Nestor, Menelaos and Helen. We hear Odysseus' own memories in Books IX–XII, and various fabricated ones in the poem's second half. It also happens in a more formal setting. The bards Phemios and Demodokos sing songs which, though not drawn from their own experiences, are founded in collective memory, and provoke reminiscence in others.

II

The *Odyssey* is concerned with the collision of cultures. Odysseus frequently, and sometimes disastrously, attempts to forge connections with figures at the fringes of the known world: Polyphemos, the Lotuseaters, the Laistrygones. In the underworld, Teiresias, when predicting Odysseus' future, tells him that he will continue to travel and meet alien people after he has defeated the suitors (XI.119–31). It is in his nature to explore.

The range of Odysseus' wanderings is phenomenal, especially when we consider how circumscribed the life of the poet is likely to have been. (There is no way of proving that the *Odyssey* wasn't composed by a globe-trotting bard, but it seems improbable.) The poem is an amalgam of folk tales and scraps of genuine (but secondhand, and therefore potentially inaccurate) geographical information. After all, many of the places mentioned (particularly in Odysseus' narration) do not correspond to actual places – and those that do are often hazy when it comes to detail (this is one reason why searches to discover the 'real' Ithaka are doomed to failure). It may be that the account of Odysseus' wanderings adapts or incorporates reports of Greek travellers and settlers beginning to reach the outer edges of the Black Sea and Mediterranean – and some scholars have argued that Odysseus is best seen as a 'hero of protocolonization' (Malkin 1998: 10).

These encounters – with strange people and monsters – help to define Odysseus and the world from which he comes. This is, above all, an agricultural world – as indicated by the nature of the ploughman simile quoted above. Odysseus and his men behave in a way which reveals their agricultural origins: they grow grain (twice described as 'men's marrow', at II.290 and XX.108), and eat bread; they work the land, and sacrifice cattle to the gods (a necessary prelude to eating meat). When they first approach the Cyclops' island, Odysseus instinctively sees it in terms of its susceptibility to cultivation – and, by implication, colonisation. His subsequent encounter with Polyphemos can be seen in colonial terms (see on Book IX below). Odysseus' first acknowledgement that the encounter is developing badly comes when he describes the Cyclops as 'not / like a man, an eater of bread' (IX.190–1). It is significant that when the survivors make it back onto the boat, they sacrifice the sheep they have stolen – an assertion of the Greek cultural practices despised by Polyphemos. Equally, Kalypso's island – with its fairytale atmosphere and 'meadows growing soft with parsley / and violets' is alien and inhospitable to Odysseus precisely because agriculture has no place there. Hermes grumbles, when he travels there to insist on Odysseus' release, that 'there is no city of men nearby, nor people / who offer choice hecatombs to the gods, and perform sacrifice' (V.101–2). The urge to sacrifice even lies behind the most impious act of the poem: the slaughter of Helios' cattle (XII.352–65). When Odysseus' men do this (as their leader sleeps) they observe every aspect of the sacrificial ritual – overlooking the fact that they are stealing from a god, rather than honouring him.

Some readers have been appalled by the apparent emphasis placed on food in the *Odyssey*, and regarded Odysseus himself as a gluttonous figure; the 'Separatists' regarded the varied diet described in the poem as one reason it could not have been written by the poet of the *Iliad* (see Heath 2000). There is even a gastronomic parody of the *Odyssey*, dating from about 350 BC. Its author, Matro of Pitane, uses Homeric language to describe a great feast, and opens the poem *deipna moi ennepe, Mousa* ... ('Tell me, Muse, of the dinners . . .'), rather than *andra moi ennepe, Mousa* . . . (Tell me, Muse, of the man . . .) (see Olson and Sens 1999). In fact, Odysseus has an extremely conservative view of diet, and yearns to return to the world of bread, sacrifice, and land (see Vidal-Naquet 1996).

The other central cultural expectation that Odysseus takes with him wherever he goes is that people will abide by the laws of hospitality, or guest friendship (Gk *xeinia*). That is to say, he imagines that wherever he goes he will be welcomed and entertained, that he will not have to reveal his identity until he has enjoyed hospitality, and that he will be presented with 'guest gifts'. We see this system working well for Telemachos in Books II–IV, when he visits Nestor and Menelaos. It rarely works for Odysseus during the first half of the poem (his stay with the Phaiakians is the exception), because he is on the very fringes of the Greek world. He makes the terrible mistake of assuming that the Cyclops Polyphemos will respect the laws of guest friendship, but the Cyclops has no intention of doing so. Indeed, he mocks Odysseus' naivety, and tells him that his 'guest present' is being the last man to be eaten (IX.369–70). The episode is wonderfully echoed later in the poem, when the arrogant suitor Ktesippos throws an ox-foot at the head of the disguised Odysseus, and declares it to be a 'guest gift' (XX.296). The remark glances back to Odysseus' time in the Cyclops' cave, and reveals the suitor to be less than human – preparing the way for the bloodletting that is to follow. Humanity is defined by adherence to a set of essentially Greek cultural practices, which are typically rejected by alien peoples; natives of Ithaka, though, can also exclude themselves.

III

Odysseus is an unusual hero, and this lends the poem much of its distinctive flavour. He is cunning, or crafty – but his craftiness (Gk *mētis*) often shades into deceit. He spends much of the *Odyssey* concealing his true identity: he is 'Nobody' to the Cyclops, he is elusive on arrival in Phaiakia, and when back in Ithaka he disguises himself as a beggar, and assumes five separate (but overlapping) identities. This behaviour is in keeping with the Odysseus of the Troy story – the Odysseus who came up with the idea of the wooden horse, and accomplished through an ingenious trick what the Greek army had failed to do in a ten-year siege. (Odysseus is so proud of this that he asks Demodokos to sing about it at VIII.492–8.) His escape from Polyphemos' cave is an inversion of the wooden horse trick. Again, he conceals himself in animal form – but this time to escape destruction rather than inflict it.

Odysseus can display martial prowess when it is required of him. We know this from the *Iliad* (XI.395–484), and it is also displayed at the close of the *Odyssey*, when he and three supporters take on the whole mass of suitors. But more often in this poem the complex and ambiguous situations in which he is placed do not encourage (or allow) prowess in battle. On the Scherian coast he meets a young girl, and has no idea whether she is mortal or a goddess, benign or hostile. He has the further disadvantage of being naked. He handles the situation perfectly. Similarly, in the Cyclops' cave, an excessive display of force would be unwise. A hero such as Aias, the bravest and most headstrong of the Greek warriors at Troy, might have killed Polyphemos after blinding him – and subsequently starved to death. Odysseus realises that he needs to harness Polyphemos' strength in order to get out; his 'second thought' stays him (IX.302).

Nor does Odysseus *look* like a normal hero; he may be 'god-like' but the resemblance is primarily mental; he is after all 'the equal of Zeus in counsel' (*Iliad* II.169). His unheroic appearance is first attested in the *Iliad*, when Helen and Antenor are watching him from the Trojan battlements; Antenor asks who this strange man is, 'shorter in truth by a head than Atreus' son Agamemnon / . . . . / Truly, to some deep-fleeced ram would I liken him', III.193–7. And we also get a sense of his diminutive stature from Polyphemos' baffled reaction when he realises that Odysseus – and not some statuesque hero – is the man destined to defeat him:

> But always I was on the lookout for a man handsome
> and tall, with great endowment of strength on him, to come here;
> but now the end of it is that a little man, niddering, feeble,
> has taken away the sight of my eye, first making me helpless
> with wine (IX.513–17)

And, of course, for almost all of books XIII–XXIII, Odysseus is old, wizened, and dressed in rags. He is dressed as a beggar when he performs perhaps the most conventionally heroic feat of the poem: stringing his bow and shooting an arrow through the axes (XXI.404–23).

As well as excelling in the arts of disguise and trickery – and fighting heroically when required to – Odysseus has talents which elude other heroes. Most notably, he is a gifted craftsman. When Kalypso finally allows him to leave her island, he makes his own raft from timber he has felled there. The process is described in striking detail (he 'made in addition a steering oar by which to direct her, / and fenced her in down the whole length with wattles of osier / to keep the water out', V.255–7), which one cannot imagine being applied to any other epic hero. The same is true of his painstaking account of how he built his bed, one of its posts carved from a living tree. That bed is both an impressive artefact and a kind of trick – albeit one that is turned against him by Penelope at the moment of their reunion (see XXIII.188–204) Odysseus' craftsmanship is, in part, an aspect of his *mētis*; his ability to craft a boat or bed corresponds to his ability to craft a story.

IV

The *Odyssey* is a poem with a domestic focus. The *Iliad* is about a decade-long struggle, by the greatest army in human history, to topple a mighty civilisation – or, at least, it is set in the context of that struggle. The *Odyssey* is concerned with something smaller, and more readily intelligible – a decade-long struggle by one man to get home to his wife and son, resisting temptations and escaping dangers. It is hardly surprising that, even if the *Iliad* has more often been judged the better poem, it is the *Odyssey* which is far more regularly imitated by novelists and film-makers.

The *Iliad* is concerned almost entirely with the actions of great and warlike men. This is not true of the *Odyssey*, which has the most diverse cast of characters imaginable. We meet, during Odysseus' narration, a number of divine or supernatural beings. Warriors familiar from the *Iliad* reappear, during Telamachos' travels and Odysseus' *nekuia* (or, visit to the underworld). But, more significantly still, we are introduced during the Ithakan sections of the poem to the full social spectrum. We meet slaves such as Eumaios, Philoitios and Eurykleia, alongside the haughty, aristocratic suitors and Odysseus' own family. And we are forced by the manner of Odysseus' return to consider the way in which the social classes interact: for a substantial part of the poem, its hero is disguised – and treated – as a beggar. This has led some critics to suggest that the *Odyssey* should be read as a critique of the social order (although this raises the further question of which social order is being scrutinised). (See: Rose 1975; Farron 1979–80; Thalmann 1998.)

The poem's tone and subject matter are equally down-to-earth. There are plenty of episodes in the *Odyssey* which would never have found their way into an epic poem by Virgil or Milton (who despite their veneration of Homer had very definite ideas about the propriety of epic).

Eumaios' hut, to give one example, is described in painstaking detail – just as carefully, in fact, as Odysseus' palace (XIV.5–28). And consider the moment when Odysseus – still dressed as a beggar – meets his old dog Argos:

> There the dog Argos lay in the dung, all covered with dog ticks.
> Now, as he perceived that Odysseus had come close to him,
> he wagged his tail, and laid both his ears back. (XVII.300–2)

In Pope's version (published 1725–6), we might note, the grubby detail is suppressed:

> Thus, near the gates conferring as they drew,
> Argus, the Dog, his ancient master knew;
> He, not unconscious of the voice, and tread,
> Lifts to the sound his ear, and rears his head

The accompanying note stresses the appropriateness of the detail in the original Greek: 'It is certain that the vermin which Homer mentions would debase our Poetry, but in the *Greek* that very word is noble and sonorous' – but it is significant that English notions of Epic decorum are drawn from the *Iliad* rather than the *Odyssey*.

The poem's distinctively earthy tone is most strongly felt in its similes. Extended similes are, as noted above, a central feature of Homeric epic – and one of the ways in which the poet elevates his subject matter. In the *Iliad*, warriors are regularly compared to wild animals, or natural forces: ravening lions, fast-flowing rivers, forest fires. There are moments when the points of comparison are markedly unheroic – as when the retreating Aias is compared to a donkey (XI.558). In the *Odyssey*, the objects of comparison seem far more regularly to be drawn from the poet's own world, and give a detailed sketch of life in a coastal community in (say) eighth-century Greece. When, for example, Odysseus is enduring a sleepless night, fretting about the task ahead, Homer chooses a metaphor from cookery:

> And as a man with a paunch pudding, that has been filled with
> blood and fat, tosses it back and forth over a blazing
> fire, and the pudding itself strains to be cooked quickly;
> so he was twisting and turning back and forth, meditating
> how, though he was alone against many, he could lay hands on
> the shameless suitors (XX.25–30)

In the same vein, his tunic is described as resembling the 'dried-out skin of an onion, / So sheer it was and soft, and shining bright as the sun shines' (XIX.233–4). The whirlpool Charybdis seethes 'like a cauldron over a strong fire' (XII.237)

And when we do get comparisons to the natural world, they are not always elevating in the usual Iliadic fashion. As the shipwrecked Odysseus is torn away from the Scherian coast by the undertow of a wave, he is compared to a small sea creature, discovered by fishermen:

> As when an octopus is dragged away from its shelter
> the thickly-clustered pebbles stick in the cups of the tentacles,
> so in contact with the rock the skin from his bold hands
> was torn away. (V.432–5)

When Odysseus has killed the suitors, he pauses and watches them:

> lying fallen
> in their blood and in their dust, like fish whom the fisherman
> have taken in their net with many holes, and dragged out
> onto the hollow beach from the gray sea, and all of them
> lie piled on the sand, needing the restless salt water;
> but Helios, the shining Sun, bakes the life out of them. (XXII.383–8)

The simile is evocative – and certainly helps us to imagine the suitors twitching, gulping and dying on the floor of Odysseus' great hall. But it also reveals something about the poet's situation. Markedly different in tone from anything we find in the *Iliad*, it is not just an epic simile but an Odyssean one.

Chapter 3

Selections from the *Odyssey*

The five books reproduced below, with introductions and commentary, have been chosen to give a sense of the poem's variety: in Book I Odysseus is absent and his son Telemachos is centre stage; in Book VI we see Odysseus negotiating with a strange people; Book IX is written in the first person, and is taken from the hero's own account of his adventures; Books XIII and XXIII are set on Ithaka, as Odysseus struggles to regain control of his household. Readers new to the poem are strongly advised to read these selections in conjunction with the summary of the poem on pp. 6–11 above.

Book I: Telemachos and Athene

The *Odyssey* opens – as epic poems tend to – with a *proem*, or introductory passage, in which the singer appeals to the Muse and lays out a prospectus for the narrative that will follow. Like the epic it introduces, this proem delays the arrival of its hero. The poem's first word tells us that it will be about a man (Gk *andra*), but it is not until line 21, just before we embark on the narrative proper, that we are told it will concern 'godlike Odysseus'. In other respects, the proem is a misleading guide to the narrative ahead. It gives undue prominence to the consumption of Helios' cattle, and it deals with Odysseus' exploits in Ithaka (the entire second half of the poem) in a couple of lines. In particular, the poet (or the Muse) also seems strangely keen to absolve Odysseus of responsibility for the death of his men – most of whom were already dead by the time the one remaining ship reaches Helios' island.

Odysseus is the very last Greek warrior to return from Troy; the story opens at a time when 'all the others, as many as fled sheer destruction, / were at home now, having escaped the sea and the fighting' (I.11–12). In the background to the *Odyssey* hover various homecomings which have already taken place. In Book IV Telemachos will meet the Spartan prince Menelaos and his wife Helen – whose elopement with Paris was the initial reason for the Trojan expedition. They are back in the comfort of their palace, and when Telemachos visits them there they reminisce about the exploits of various Greeks – Odysseus among them.

Odysseus will also be confronted with tales of other homecomings, during the *nekuia* (visit to the underworld) in Book XI, when he speaks to the ghosts of fallen comrades. Inevitably, given the context for his discussions, some of these returns have been unhappy ones. In particular, that of Agamemnon, the leader of the Greek expedition, has been ill-fated. Having survived the war and the voyage home, he was murdered by his wife and her lover – and has these words for Odysseus:

> You have been present in your time at the slaughter of many
> men, killed singly, or in the strong encounters of battle;
> but beyond all others you would have been sorry at heart
> for this scene, how we lay sprawled by the mixing bowl and the
>   loaded
> tables, all over the palace, and the whole floor was steaming
> with blood. (XI.416–21)

Why should Odysseus have been particularly sorry at heart to see this scene? Not out of any great love for Agamemnon, but because he fears that a similar fate might await him. When he finally returns to Ithaka, there is indeed a battle at a banquet – and a death which closely resembles that of Agamemnon:

> he, sprawling over the table,
> doubled and fell, and on the floor the good food was scattered,
> and the two-handed goblet (XXII.84–6)

In fact, the killer here is Odysseus, and the unhappy diner is Eurylochos, the suitors' ringleader. But the account in Book XXII is a thrilling near-fulfilment of the anxiety which begins in the very first book. The first story told in the *Odyssey* is Zeus' account of the fall-out from Agamemnon's murder – how Orestes avenged his father's death by killing Aigisthos – and the story is alluded to throughout the poem.

The example of Agamemnon's return plays a crucial role in the first book of the *Odyssey*. We wonder, of course, whether Odysseus' fate will be similar to Agamemnon's – and he presumably wonders whether Penelope will prove to be another Klytaimestra. (And perhaps versions of the story did exist in which Odysseus returned to an unfaithful wife, or was over-powered by her suitors; we know only that this is not the only version, and cannot possibly tell to what extent the variants differed.) But the character on whom this background narrative weighs most heavily is Telemachos, who is, at the start of the poem, an inexperienced and somewhat callow youth, and whose development is charted in the first four books. Zeus remarks, rather pointedly, that Orestes was only able to exact vengeance when 'he had come of age'. Athene, disguised as Mentes, makes the point directly, when she visits Ithaka:

> You should not go on
> clinging to your childhood. You are no longer of an age to do that.
> Or have you not heard what glory was won by great Orestes
> among all mankind, when he killed the murderer of his father . . . ?
>   (I.296–9)

We wonder, naturally, when and whether Telemachos will be ready to participate fully in the action of this song – to assist his father, or (if necessary) to avenge him. Orestes' role might be compared to that of Fortinbras in *Hamlet*: a much-praised man of action, acting as a foil to the wavering prince.

The first four books of the *Odyssey* are often referred to as the *Telemacheia*, and Odysseus' absence will come as a surprise to many first-time readers of the *Odyssey*. Having promised to sing of 'the man of many ways', the poet leaves him to his own devices for a sixth of the poem and instead focuses on his son. This structural quirk has also been a stumbling block for many scholars – specifically for *analysts* (see p. 102 below), who have proposed that it may be the result of two entirely separate poems being grafted together: one dealing with Telemachos' travels, another with his father's return. The objection is unnecessary, since the first four books of the poem work brilliantly in two respects. First, they show us the sorry state of affairs in Ithaka, and impress upon us the urgent need for Odysseus' return. Second, they show us the start of Telemachos' moral and emotional development – which will come to fruition in the final books of the *Odyssey*. And the *Telemacheia* also meshes perfectly with, and anticipates beautifully, the poem's later stages. When we first meet Telemachos, he is day-dreaming – envisaging, as it happens, precisely the sequence of events with which the poem ends:

> imagining in his mind his great father, how he might come back
> and all throughout the house might cause the suitors to scatter,
> and hold his rightful place and be lord of his own possessions. (115–17)

In one important respect, Telemachos is already a greater man than the suitors who fill his father's palace. He displays a sound understanding of the laws surrounding *xeinia* (or 'guest-friendship'), which were of central importance in the Greek world. When he first sees a stranger, the Taphian Mentes (in fact, Athene in disguise), Telemachos' first impulse is to offer hospitality, refusing to ask his guest any questions until he has eaten. The laws of hospitality are central to the *Odyssey* – Odysseus will appeal to them, with varying degrees of success when dealing with the Cyclops, with the Phaiakians, and with his own compatriots – and their importance is firmly established in the first book.

Tell me, Muse, of the man of many ways*, who was driven
far journeys, after he had sacked* Troy's sacred citadel.
Many were they whose cities he saw, whose minds he learned of,
many the pains he suffered in his spirit on the wide sea,
struggling for his own life and the homecoming of his companions.   5
Even so he could not save his companions, hard though
he strove to; they were destroyed by their own wild recklessness,*
fools, who devoured the oxen of Helios, the Sun God,
and he took away the day of their homecoming. From some point
here, goddess, daughter of Zeus, speak, and begin our story.   10
     Then all the others, as many as fled sheer destruction,
were at home now, having escaped the sea and the fighting.
This one alone, longing for his wife and his homecoming,
was detained by the queenly nymph Kalypso, bright among
     goddesses,
in her hollowed caverns, desiring that he should be her husband.   15
But when in the circling of the years that very year came
in which the gods had spun for him his time of homecoming
to Ithaka, not even then was he free of his trials
nor among his own people. But all the gods pitied him
except Poseidon; he remained relentlessly angry   20
with godlike Odysseus*, until his return to his own country.
     But Poseidon was gone now to visit the far Aithiopians,
Aithiopians*, most distant of men, who live divided,
some at the setting of Hyperion*, some at his rising,

---

1 **the man of many ways**] Man (Gk *andra*) is the first word of the poem in Greek. The Greek word *polutropos* can mean both cunning (of many tricks) and well-travelled (of many journeys).
    2 **sacked**] Odysseus came up with the idea of the wooden horse, and was the leader of the Greek soldiers hidden inside it. See VIII.499–520.
    7 **destroyed by their own wild recklessness**] This is inaccurate. Odysseus leaves Troy with twelve ships, and eleven of them have already been destroyed (by the man-eating Laistrygones) before they encounter Helios' cattle.
    21 **godlike Odysseus**] The hero's name is delayed until the end of the proem.
    23 **Aithiopians**] There are, in this account, two distinct groups of Aithiopians, eastern and western, and it is unclear which group Poseidon is visiting.
    24 **Hyperion**] The sun.

to receive a hecatomb* of bulls and rams. There   25
he sat at the feast and took his pleasure. Meanwhile the other
Olympian gods were gathered together in the halls of Zeus.
First among them to speak was the father of gods and mortals,
for he was thinking in his heart of stately Aigisthos,
whom Orestes, Agamemnon's far-famed son, had murdered.   30
Remembering him he spoke now before the immortals:
    'Oh for shame, how the mortals put the blame upon us
gods, for they say evils come from us, but it is they, rather,
who by their own recklessness win sorrow beyond what is given,
as lately, beyond what was given, Aigisthos married   35
the wife of Atreus' son,* and murdered him on his homecoming,
though he knew it was sheer destruction, for we ourselves had told
    him,
sending Hermes, the mighty watcher, Argeïphontes,*
not to kill the man, nor court his lady in marriage;
for vengeance would come on him from Orestes, son of Atreides,   40
whenever he came of age and longed for his own country.
So Hermes told him, but for all his kind intention he could not
persuade the mind of Aigisthos. And now he has paid for
    everything.'
    Then in turn the goddess gray-eyed Athene* answered him:
'Son of Kronos,* our father, O lordliest of the mighty,   45
Aigisthos indeed has been struck down in a death well merited.
Let any other man who does thus perish as he did.
But the heart in me is torn for the sake of wise Odysseus,
unhappy man, who still, far from his friends, is suffering
griefs, on the sea-washed island, the navel of all the waters,   50
a wooded island, and there a goddess has made her dwelling place;
she is the daughter of malignant Atlas,* who has discovered
all the depths of the sea, and himself sustains the towering
columns which bracket earth and sky and hold them together.

---

25 **hecatomb**] A sacrifice – but literally, a hundred cattle, from the Greek *hekaton* (hundred) and *bous* (oxen).

36 **Atreus' son**] Agamemnon. His brother Menelaos is also referred to in this way, at (e.g.) IV.185. Agamemnon's wife, Klytaimestra, took Aigisthos as a lover while her husband was commanding the Greek forces at Troy.

38 **Argeïphontes**] This traditional epithet of Hermes means 'the dog-slayer'. Hermes killed Argos, the hundred-eyed dog who guarded Io (see Graves 1960: 56a). The epithet may also refer to Hermes' role as the god of thieves, responsible for killing the guard-dog.

44 **Athene**] Goddess of war, and associated with cunning intelligence. She features prominently in the *Odyssey* as Odysseus' greatest supporter.

45 **Son of Kronos**] Zeus.

52 **Atlas**] The titan whose task is to prevent the heavens from collapsing into the sea, by holding up the sky – a punishment for rebelling against Zeus. He is the father of Kalypso, the nymph currently detaining Odysseus.

This is his daughter; she detains the grieving, unhappy 55
man, and ever with soft and flattering words she works to
charm him to forget Ithaka; and yet Odysseus,
straining to get sight of the very smoke uprising
from his own country, longs to die.* But you, Olympian,
the heart in you is heedless of him. Did not Odysseus 60
do you grace by the ships of the Argives, making sacrifice
in wide Troy? Why, Zeus, are you now so harsh with him?'
    Then in turn Zeus who gathers the clouds made answer:
'My child, what sort of word escaped your teeth's barrier?
How could I forget Odysseus the godlike, he who 65
is beyond all other men in mind, and who beyond others
has given sacrifice to the gods, who hold wide heaven?
It is the Earth Encircler Poseidon who, ever relentless,
nurses a grudge because of the Cyclops, whose eye he blinded;
for Polyphemos like a god,* whose power is greatest 70
over all the Cyclopes. Thoösa, a nymph, was his mother,
and she was daughter of Phorkys, lord of the barren salt water.
She in the hollows of the caves had lain with Poseidon.
For his sake Poseidon, shaker of the earth, although he does not
kill Odysseus, yet drives him back from the land of his fathers. 75
But come, let all of us who are here work out his homecoming
and see to it that he returns. Poseidon shall put away
his anger; for all along and against the will of the other
immortal gods united he can accomplish nothing.'
    Then, in turn, the goddess gray-eyed Athene answered him: 80
'Son of Kronos, our father, O lordliest of the mighty,
if in truth this is pleasing to the blessed immortals
that Odysseus of the many designs shall return home, then
let us dispatch Hermes, the guide, the slayer of Argos,
to the island of Ogygia, so that with all speed 85
he may announce to the lovely-haired nymph our absolute purpose,
the homecoming of enduring Odysseus, that he shall come back.
But I shall make my way to Ithaka, so that I may
stir up his son a little, and put some confidence in him
to summon into assembly the flowing-haired Achaians 90
and make a statement to all the suitors, who now forever
slaughter his crowding sheep and lumbering horn-curved cattle;
and I will convey him into Sparta and to sandy Pylos

---

59 **longs to die**] The sequence here is confusing. Odysseus' longing for death presumably stems from despair, although he is still 'straining' to reach home. When in Phaiakia, he expresses the opposite idea: 'let life leave me when I have once / seen my property' (VII.224–5).
70 **Polyphemos like a god**] Note that the Cyclops, like Odysseus (I.21) is described as godlike (Gk *antitheos*). The epithet implies strength and importance, rather than moral standing.

to ask after his dear father's homecoming, if he can hear something,
and so that among people he may win a good reputation.'   95
   Speaking so she bound upon her feet the fair sandals,
golden and immortal, that carried her over the water
as over the dry boundless earth abreast of the wind's blast.
Then she caught up a powerful spear, edged with sharp bronze,
heavy, huge, thick, wherewith she beats down the battalions of
   fighting   100
men, against whom she of the mighty father is angered,
and descended in a flash of speed from the peaks of Olympos,
and lighted in the land of Ithaka, at the doors of Odysseus
at the threshold of the court, and in her hand was the bronze spear.
She was disguised as a friend, leader of the Taphians,* Mentes.   105
There she found the haughty suitors. They at the moment
in front of the doors were amusing their spirits with draughts games,*
sitting about on skins of cattle whom they had slaughtered
themselves, and about them, of their heralds and hard-working
   henchmen,
some at the mixing bowls* were combining wine and water,   110
while others again with porous sponges were wiping the tables
and setting them out, and others were cutting meat in quantities.
   Now far the first to see Athene was godlike Telemachos,*
as he sat among the suitors, his heart deep grieving within him,
imagining in his mind his great father, how he might come back   115
and all throughout the house might cause the suitors to scatter,
and hold his rightful place and be lord of his own possessions.
With such thoughts, sitting among the suitors, he saw Athene
and went straight to the forecourt, the heart within him scandalized
that a guest should still be standing at the doors. He stood beside her 120
and took her by the right hand, and relieved her of her bronze spear,
and spoke to her and addressed her in winged words: 'Welcome,
   stranger.
You shall be entertained as a guest among us. Afterward,
when you have tasted dinner, you shall tell us what your need is.'

---

105 **disguised . . . Taphians**] Gods frequently disguise themselves when appearing to mortals in the *Odyssey* (see also XIII.221–6), whereas in the *Iliad* they tend to appear as themselves. (A notable exception is the appearance of Hermes to Priam at *Iliad* XXIV.339–467 – though he eventually reveals himself.)

107 **draughts games**] Homer describes the suitors as playing with pebbles (Gk *pessoisi*), but what they are doing with them is unclear. A later tradition (recorded by Athenaeus, among others) has them playing a game called Penelope in which each of the 108 suitors (the number is unattested in Homer) threw a pebble at a central pebble, which they called 'the Penelope'.

110 **mixing bowls**] Wine was almost always diluted in the ancient world, and the process of dilution was an important element in the ritual of drinking.

113 **Telemachos**] His name means 'skilful at archery', but the skill referred to is presumably his father's, whose ability with a bow is central to the plot of the poem.

So speaking he led the way, and Pallas Athene followed him.   125
Now, when the two of them were inside the lofty dwelling,
he took the spear and carried and set it against a tall column
in a rack for spears, of polished wood, where indeed there were other
spears of patient-hearted Odysseus standing in numbers,
and he led her and seated her in a chair, with a cloth to sit on,   130
the chair splendid and elaborate. For her feet there was a footstool.
For himself, he drew a painted bench next her, apart from the others,
the suitors, for fear the guest, made uneasy by the uproar,
might lose his appetite there among overbearing people,
and so he might also ask him about his absent father.   135
A maidservant brought water for them* and poured it from a splendid
and golden pitcher, holding it above a silver basin
for them to wash, and she pulled a polished table before them.
A grave housekeeper brought in the bread and served it to them,
adding many good things to it, generous with her provisions,   140
while a carver lifted platters of all kinds of meats and set them
in front of them, and placed beside them the golden goblets,
and a herald, going back and forth, poured the wine for them.
    Then the haughty suitors came in, and all of them straightway
took their places in order on chairs and along the benches,   145
and their heralds poured water over their hands for them to wash with,
and the serving maids brought them bread heaped up in the baskets,
and the young men filled the mixing bowls with wine for their drinking.
They put their hands to the good things that lay ready before them.
But when they had put away their desire for eating and drinking,   150
the suitors found their attention turned to other matters,
the song and the dance; for these things come at the end of feasting.
A herald put the beautifully wrought lyre in the hands
of Phemios, who sang for the suitors,* because they made him.
He played his lyre and struck up a fine song. Meanwhile   155
Telemachos talked to Athene of the gray eyes, leaning

136–42 Sections from this passage are repeated almost word-for-word at IV.52–8; VII.172–6; X.368–72; XV.135–9; and XVII.91–5. The re-use of passages of verse is a feature of oral poetry (on which, see under 'Contexts' below). It is particularly common in descriptions of ritual activity – sacrifice, feasting, drinking, hospitality – in which actions follow a pre-ordained pattern.

153–5 It is tempting to imagine that the *Iliad* and *Odyssey* would have been composed and performed in circumstances similar to these. The lyre (Gk *phorminx*) would have been made from a tortoise shell, which acted as the sound box, and a pair of ox horns. A cross-bar was fixed between the horns, and the strings of the instrument stretched to the base of the shell.

his head close to hers, so that none of the others might hear him:
'Dear stranger, would you be scandalized at what I say to you?
This is all they think of, the lyre and the singing. Easy
for them, since without penalty they eat up the substance   160
of a man whose white bones lie out in the rain and fester
somewhere on the mainland, or roll in the wash of the breakers.
If they were ever to see him coming back to Ithaka
all the prayer of them all would be to be lighter on their feet
instead of to be richer men for gold and clothing.   165
As it is, he has died by an evil fate, and there is no comfort
left for us, not even though some one among mortals
tells us he will come back. His day of homecoming has perished.
But come now, tell me this and give me an accurate answer.
What man are you, and whence? Where is your city? Your parents?   170
What kind of ship did you come here on? And how did the sailors
bring you to Ithaka? What men do they claim that they are?
For I do not think you could have traveled on foot* to this country.
And tell me this too, tell me truly, so that I may know it.
Are you here for the first time, or are you a friend of my father's   175
from abroad? Since many other men too used to come and visit
our house, in the days when he used to go about among people.'
    Then in turn the goddess gray-eyed Athene answered him:
'See, I will accurately* answer all that you ask me.
I announce myself as Mentes, son of Anchialos   180
the wise, and my lordship is over the oar-loving Taphians.
Now I have come in as you see, with my ship and companions
sailing over the wine-blue water to men of alien language.
to Temese, after bronze, and my cargo is gleaming iron.
And my ship stands near by, at the country, away from the city,   185
at the harbor, Rheithron, underneath wooded Neion.
Your father and I claim to be guest-friends by heredity*
from far back, as you would know if you went to the aged hero
Laertes,* who, they say, no longer comes to the city
now, but away by himself on his own land leads a hard life   190
with an old woman to look after him, who serves him his victuals

---

173 **travelled on foot**] Could this be a joke? Ithaka is an island. Telemachos asks the same question (this time of the disguised Odysseus) at XVI.59.

179 **accurately**] The account that follows is far from accurate. Athene deliberately misleads Telemachos at various points (see the close of Book XIII).

187 **guest-friends by heredity**] The reciprocity associated with guest-friendships is cross-generational. So there is nothing odd in Telemachos extending a warm welcome to 'Mentes', even though they have never met. Mentes' false claim is echoed by Odysseus himself at XIX.185, who claims, when posing as a Cretan nobleman, to have entertained Odysseus twenty years earlier.

189 **Laertes**] Odysseus' elderly father, who was a great hero in his youth (he was one of the Argonauts who accompanied Jason in his quest for the Golden Fleece (see Graves 1960: 48i). He does not appear in the *Odyssey* until the final book of the poem.

and drink, at the times when the weariness has befallen his body
from making his toilsome way on the high ground of his vineyard.
Now I have come. They told me he was here in this country,
your father, I mean. But no. The gods are impeding his passage.   195
For no death on the land has befallen the great Odysseus,
but somewhere, alive on the wide sea, he is held captive,
on a sea-washed island, and savage men have him in their keeping,*
rough men, who somehow keep him back, though he is unwilling.
Now, I will make you a prophecy, in the way the immortals   200
put it into my mind, and as I think it will come out,
though I am no prophet,* nor do I know the ways of birds clearly.
He will not long be absent from the beloved land of his fathers,
even if the bonds that hold him are iron, but he will be thinking
of a way to come back, since he is a man of many resources.   205
But come now tell me this and give me an accurate answer.
Are you, big as you are, the very child of Odysseus?
Indeed, you are strangely like about the head, the fine eyes,
as I remember; we used to meet so often together
before he went away to Troy, where others beside him   210
and the greatest of the Argives went in their hollow vessels.
Since that time I have not seen Odysseus nor he has seen me.'
    Then the thoughtful Telemachos said to her in answer:
'See, I will accurately answer all that you ask me.
My mother says indeed I am his. I for my part   215
do not know. Nobody really knows his own father.
But how I wish I could have been rather son to some fortunate
man, whom old age overtook among his possessions.
But of mortal men, that man has proved the most ill-fated
whose son they say I am: since you question me on this matter.'   220
    Then in turn the goddess gray-eyed Athene answered him:
'The gods have not made yours a birth that will go nameless
hereafter, since Penelope bore such a son as you are.
But come now, tell me this and give me an accurate answer.
What feast is this, what gathering? How does it concern you?   225
A festival, or a wedding? Surely, no communal dinner.
How insolently they seem to swagger about in their feasting
all through the house. A serious man who came in among them
could well be scandalized, seeing much disgraceful behavior.'
    Then the thoughtful Telemachos said to her in answer: 230
'My guest, since indeed you are asking me all these questions,
there was a time this house was one that might be prosperous

---

198 **savage men have him in their keeping**] As Athene knows, Odysseus is being detained by a
female demi-god, and not by a group of savage men.
    202 **I am no prophet**] A misleading piece of truth-telling. She is a goddess.

and above reproach, when a certain man was here in his country.
But now the gods, with evil intention, have willed it otherwise,
and they have caused him to disappear, in a way no other   235
man has done. I should not have sorrowed so over his dying
if he had gone down among his companions in the land of the Trojans,
or in the arms of his friends, after he had wound up the fighting.
So all the Achaians would have heaped a grave mound over him,
and he would have won great fame for himself and his son hereafter. 240
But now ingloriously the stormwinds have caught and carried him
away, out of sight, out of knowledge, and he left pain and
   lamentation
to me. Nor is it for him alone that I grieve in my pain now.
No longer. For the gods have inflicted other cares on me.
For all the greatest men who have the power in the islands,   245
in Douchilion and Same and in wooded Zakynthos,
and all who in rocky Ithaka are holders of lordships,
all these are after my mother for marriage, and wear my house out.
And she does not refuse the hateful marriage, nor is she able
to make an end of the matter; and these eating up my substance   250
waste it away; and soon they will break me myself to pieces.'
   Pallas Athene answered him in great indignation:
'Oh, for shame. How great your need is now of the absent
Odysseus, who would lay his hands on these shameless suitors.
I wish he could come now to stand in the outer doorway   255
of his house, wearing a helmet and carrying shield and two spears,
the way he was the first time that ever I saw him
in our own house, drinking his wine and taking his pleasure,
coming in from Ephyre and from Ilos son of Mermeros.
Odysseus, you see, had gone there also in his swift ship   260
in search of a poison to kill men, so he might have it
to smear on his bronze-headed arrows, but Ilos would not
give him any, since he feared the gods who endure forever.
But my father did give it to him, so terribly did he love him.
I wish that such an Odysseus would come now among the suitors.   265
They would all find death was quick, and marriage a painful
   matter.*
Yet all these things that are lying upon the gods' knees:
whether he will come home to his vengeance, here in his household,
or whether he will not. Rather I will urge you to consider
some means by which you can force the suitors out of your
   household.   270

265–6 **I wish . . . matter**] Menelaos says exactly the same thing when Telemachos visits him to ask for advice (IV.345–6).

Come now, pay close attention to me and do as I tell you.*
Tomorrow, summon the Achaian warriors into assembly
and publish your word to all, let the gods be your witnesses.
Tell the suitors to scatter and go back to their own holdings,
and as for your mother, if the spirit urges her to be married,   275
let her go back to the palace of her powerful father,
and they shall appoint the marriage and arrange for the wedding
    presents
in great amount, as ought to go with a beloved daughter.
But for yourself, I will counsel you shrewdly, and hope you will
    listen.
Fit out a ship with twenty oars, the best you can come by,   280
and go out to ask about your father who is so long absent,
on the chance some mortal man can tell you, who has listened to
    Rumor
sent by Zeus. She more than others spreads news among people.
First go to Pylos, and there question the great Nestor,
and from there go over to Sparta to see fair-haired Menelaos,   285
since he came home last of all the bronze-armored Achaians.
Thus if you hear your father is alive and on his way home,
then, hard pressed though you are, you should still hold out for
    another
year. But if you hear he has died and lives no longer,
then make your way home to the beloved land of your fathers,   290
and pile up a tomb in his honor, and there make sacrifices
in great amount, as is fitting. And give your mother to a husband.
Then, after you have made an end of these matters, and done
    them,
next you must consider well in your heart and spirit
some means by which you can kill the suitors who are in your
    household,   295
by treachery or open attack. You should not go on
clinging to your childhood. You are no longer of an age to do that.
Or have you not heard what glory was won by great Orestes
among all mankind, when he killed the murderer of his father,
the treacherous Aigisthos, who had slain his famous father?*   300

271–96 This passage has been frequently argued over. Various analytical critics have held it up as evidence that the poem is the work of many hands, and that a poem about Telemachos has been crudely bolted onto the separate tale of Odysseus' return. Why – for example – does Athene / Mentes suggest first that Penelope should be married off by her father (276–7), and only sixteen lines later that her son should be responsible? Why should Telemachos give his mother to a husband and *then* attack and kill all of the suitors? The objections are summarised by Page (1955: 52–62).

298–300 Orestes' avenging of his father's murder has already been recounted at 28–43. Here the parallel is reinforced: Orestes took action when he had 'come of age'; Athene/Mentes urges Telemachos to do the same.

So you too, dear friend, since I can see you are big and splendid,
be bold also, so that in generations to come they will praise you.
But now it is time for me to go back down to my fast ship
and my companions, who must be very restless waiting
for me. Let all this be on your mind, and do as I tell you'.   305
    Then the thoughtful Telemachos said to her in answer:
'My guest, your words to me are very kind and considerate,
what any father would say to his son. I shall not forget them.
But come now, stay with me, eager though you are for your journey,
so that you may first bathe and take your ease and, well rested   310
and happy in your heart, then go back to your ship with a present,
something prized, altogether fine, which will be your keepsake
from me, what loving guests and hosts bestow on each other.'
    Then in turn the goddess gray-eyed Athene answered him:
'Do not detain me longer, eager as I am for my journey;   315
and that gift, whatever it is your dear heart bids you give me,
save it to give when I come next time, so I can take it
home; and choose a good one, and a fair exchange will befall you.'
    So spoke the goddess gray-eyed Athene, and there she departed
like a bird soaring high in the air, but she left in his spirit   320
determination and courage, and he remembered his father
even more than he had before, and guessed the meaning,
and his heart was full of wonder, for he thought it was a divinity.
At once he went over, a godlike man, to sit with the suitors.
    The famous singer was singing to them, and they in silence   325
sat listening. He sang of the Achaians' bitter homecoming*
from Troy, which Pallas Athene had inflicted upon them.
    The daughter of Ikarios, circumspect Penelope,
heard and heeded the magical song from her upper chamber,
and descended the high staircase that was built in her palace,   330
not all alone, since two handmaidens went to attend her.
When she, shining among women, came near the suitors,
she stood by the pillar that supported the roof with its joinery,
holding her shining veil in front of her face, to shield it,
and a devoted attendant was stationed on either side of her.   335
All in tears she spoke then to the divine singer:
'Phemios, since you know many other actions of mortals
and gods, which can charm men's hearts and which the singers
    celebrate,
sit beside them and sing one of these, and let them in silence

---

326 **the Achaians' bitter homecoming**] The Greek warrior Aias had raped Kassandra, the
Trojan prophetess, while she sought refuge at the statue of Athene. As a result, Athene cursed the
Greeks with a difficult journey home. This does not apply to Odysseus, whose homecoming she is
trying to expedite – though Penelope is of course unaware of this.

go on drinking their wine, but leave off singing this sad   340
song, which always afflicts the dear heart deep inside me,
since the unforgettable sorrow comes to me, beyond others,
so dear a head do I long for whenever I am reminded
of my husband, whose fame goes wide through Hellas and midmost
    Argos.'
    Then the thoughtful Telemachos said to her in answer: 345
'Why, my mother, do you begrudge this excellent singer
his pleasing himself as the thought drives him? It is not the singers
who are to blame, it must be Zeus is to blame, who gives out
to men who eat bread, to each and all, the way he wills it.
There is nothing wrong in his singing the sad return of the Danaans.   350
People, surely, always give more applause to that song
which is the latest to circulate among the listeners.
So let your heart and let your spirit be hardened to listen.
Odysseus is not the only one who lost his homecoming
day at Troy. There were many others who perished, besides him.   355
Go therefore back in the house, and take up your own work,
the loom and the distaff, and see to it that your handmaidens
ply their work also; but the men must see to discussion,
all men, but I most of all. For mine is the power in this household.'
    Penelope went back inside the house, in amazement,   360
for she laid the serious words of her son deep away in her spirit,
and she went back to the upper story with her attendant
women, and wept for Odysseus, her beloved husband, until
gray-eyed Athene cast sweet slumber over her eyelids.
    But the suitors all through the shadowy halls were raising a
    tumult,   365
and all prayed for the privilege of lying beside her,
until the thoughtful Telemachos began speaking among them:
'You suitors of my mother, overbearing in your rapacity,
now let us dine and take our pleasure, and let there be no
shouting, since it is a splendid thing to listen to a singer   370
who is such a singer as this man is, with a voice such as gods have.
Then tomorrow let us all go to the place of assembly,
and hold a session, where I will give you my forthright statement,
that you go out of my palace and do your feasting elsewhere,
eating up your own possessions, taking turns, household by
    household.   375
But if you decide it is more profitable and better
to go on, eating up one man's livelihood, without payment,
then spoil my house. I will cry out to the gods everlasting
in the hope that Zeus might somehow grant a reversal of fortunes.
Then you may perish in this house, with no payment given.'   380

So he spoke, and all of them bit their lips in amazement
at Telemachos and the daring way he had spoken to them.
    It was Antinoös* the son of Eupeithes who answered:
'Telemachos, surely it must be the very gods who prompt you
to take the imperious line and speak so daringly to us.   385
I hope the son of Kronos never makes you our king* in seagirt
Ithaka. Though to be sure that is your right by inheritance.'
    Then the thoughtful Telemachos said to him in answer:
'Antinoös, in case you wonder at what I am saying,
I would be willing to take that right, if Zeus should give it.   390
Do you think that is the worst thing that could happen to anyone?
It is not bad to be a king. Speedily the king's house
grows prosperous, and he himself has rank beyond others.
But in fact there are many other Achaian princes,
young and old, in seagirt Ithaka, any of whom might   395
hold this position, now that the great Odysseus has perished.
But I will be the absolute lord over my own household
and my servants, whom the great Odysseus won by force for me.'
    Then in turn Eurymachos, son of Polybos, answered:
'Telemachos, these matters, and which of the Achaians will be king   400
in seagirt Ithaka, are questions that lie on the gods' knees.
But I hope you keep your possessions and stay lord in your own
    household.
May the man never come who against your will and by force shall
    drive you
away from your holdings, while Ithaka is a place still lived in.
But, best of men, I wish to ask you about this stranger,   405
where he came from, what country he announces as being
his own, where lies his parent stock, and the fields of his fathers.
Has he brought some message from your father who is on his way
    here?
Or did he arrived pursuing some matter of his own business?
How suddenly he started away and vanished, and did not   410
wait to be made known. He was no mean man, by the look of him.'
    Then the thoughtful Telemachos said to him in answer:
'Eurymachos, there is no more hope of my father's homecoming.
I believe no messages any more, even should there be one,
nor pay attention to any prophecy, those times my mother   415

383 **Antinoös**] The name means 'hostile' or 'minded against'.
386–401 The constitutional arrangements in place on Ithaka are hazy, to say the least.
Telemachos' succession does not seem to be guaranteed. The suitors – in particular, Antinoös and
Eurymachos – seem to believe that they can simply become de facto rulers by marrying Penelope
and securing control of the palace. The Greek word *basileus* can mean 'lord' or 'nobleman' as well
as 'king' – and Lattimore's translation is thus misleading.

calls some diviner into the house and asks him questions.
This stranger is a friend of my father's. He comes from Taphos
and announces himself as Mentes, the son of Anchialos
the wise. And he is lord of the lovers of the oar, the Taphians.'
   So spoke Telemachos, but in his heart he knew the immortal   420
goddess. The others, turning to the dance and the delightful
song, took their pleasure and awaited the coming of evening,
and the black evening came on as they were taking their pleasure.
Then they went home to go to bed, each to his own house,
but Telemachos went where, off the splendid courtyard, a lofty   425
bedchamber had been built for him, in his sheltered corner.
There he went to go to bed, his heart full of problems,
and devoted Eurykleia* went with him, and carried the flaring
torches. She was the daughter of Ops the son of Peisenor,
and Laertes had bought her long ago with his own possessions   430
when she was still in her first youth, and gave twenty oxen for her,
and he favored her in his house as much as his own devoted
wife, but never slept with her, for fear of his wife's anger.
She now carried the flaring torches for him. She loved him
more than the other maidservant, and had nursed him when he was
   little.   435
He opened the doors of the close-compacted bedchamber,
and sat down on the bed and took off his soft tunic
and put it into the hands of the sagacious old woman,
and she in turn folded the tunic, and took care of it for him,
and hung it up on a peg beside the corded bedstead.   440
Then she went out of the room, and pulled the door to behind her
with a silver hook, and with a strap drew home the door bolt.
There, all night long, wrapped in a soft sheepskin, he pondered
in his heart the journey that Pallas Athene had counseled.

Book VI: Odysseus and Nausikaa

Odysseus' arrival on the Scherian coast signals his return to normality
– or at least to a version of normality. Many critics have seen his stay
among the otherworldly Phaiakans as a transitional phase, between
the fairytale atmosphere of the poem's first half and his struggles to
regain his own household in the second. After various life-threatening

---

428–35 When Homer introduces a new character, however minor, he often gives us a brief
account of (or episode from) their personal history. In the *Iliad*, as we see Greek warriors fall in
battle, the narrative often breaks to tell us about the world they left behind. See, for example, *Iliad*
IV.473–81. Here the digression is of a different sort, deepening our understanding of Odysseus'
household.

encounters with non-human creatures, Odysseus finds himself among men and women again. And having spent the past seven years sharing the bed of a goddess, he is confronted by a shy (if self-possessed) young woman; his initial suggestion that Nausikaa might be a goddess might be an attempt to flatter, but could stem equally from genuine uncertainty. Nonetheless, the situation in which Odysseus finds himself is a challenging one – and illustrates neatly the different type of heroism demanded of him in the *Odyssey*. There is no possibility for him to show his skill with a weapon. He is naked, dirty, and can only rely on his famous cunning – and on the cover of a small branch. The fact that he resembles a 'ravenous lion' (the simile is close to one used in the *Iliad*) is, in this instance, a hindrance rather than a help.

At the heart of the encounter between Odysseus and Nausikaa is the practice of supplication, or *hiketeia*. To supplicate someone is to throw oneself at his or her mercy. Formally, it involves making physical contact with them (usually by grasping their knees) – although Odysseus manages to find a way around this requirement when approaching Nausikaa. Scenes of supplication occur frequently in Homer – the practice is described thirty-five times in the two epic poems – but supplication in the *Odyssey*, we might note, is of a different nature to that described in the *Iliad*. In the *Iliad*, warriors supplicate one another on the battlefield – begging to be spared death, or (failing that) for their bodies to be returned to their families. Such encounters are between two people from the same world. They may or may not establish enough of an understanding for the victor to alter his course of action – but neither party is in any doubt as to the rules of engagement (see, in particular, Burrow 1993: 15–26). In the *Odyssey*, supplication is a less regulated business. Its hero is never sure of the allegiance or identity of the people he meets, either abroad or at home – and there is an unmistakeable uncertainty (a learned uncertainty, we might think) even in his address of the slight female figure on the Scherian shore. He has good reason to be doubtful about his prospects; as he will explain later, at the Phaiakian court, his attempts to supplicate the Cyclops Polyphemos were disastrous. He supplicates Nausikaa for similar reasons; he wants to receive protection and hospitality from her, according to the laws of *xeinia*, or guest-friendship. Fortunately for him, the young princess is (like Telemachos in Book I) aware of the importance of hospitality, reminding her attendants that 'all strangers and wanderers / are sacred in the sight of Zeus' (VI.207–8).

The encounter between Odysseus and Nausikaa has, from the outset, an air of menace to it. A naked and bedraggled man approaches a young girl, away from the city – and is compared to a wild animal as he does so. But the threat of sexual violence subsides as the narrative progresses, and is replaced by the prospect of marriage. Within moments of meeting Nausikaa we are told (and she is reminded) of her marriagability (26–7). There are further references to marriage at VI.27, 66, 180, 244 and 277, and at VII.313 – the most striking of which is Nausikaa's ardent wish that 'if only the man to be called my husband could be like this one' (244). Odysseus plays on the young girl's hopes, telling her that 'nothing is better than this, more steadfast / than when two people, a man and his wife, keep a harmonious / household' (182–4). This is a typically Odyssean piece of trickiness, leading Nausikaa on while cherishing a private dream of Penelope. But the reminder of Penelope, and the 'harmonious household' to which Odysseus hopes to return, also reminds the audience that Nausikaa is another threat to the hero's *nostos*, tempting him to settle and forget. It says much about the poet's skill in characterisation – and about the flexibility allowed in oral composition, that the form of temptation presented here is so different from that posed by the other female characters who wish to marry (or at least detain and share a bed with) Odysseus. Jasper Griffin (1980a: 56–62) has written wonderfully about the care and sensitivity with which Homer distinguishes between Nausikaa, Circe, and Kalypso.

So long-suffering great Odysseus slept in that place
in an exhaustion of sleep and weariness, and now Athene
went her way to the district and city of the Phaiakian
men, who formerly lived in the spacious land, Hypereia,*
next to the Cyclopes, who were men too overbearing,*   5
and who had kept harrying them, being greater in strength. From here
godlike Nausithoös had removed and led a migration,
and settled in Scheria,* far away from men who eat bread,*
and driven a wall about the city, and built the houses,
and made the temple of the gods, and allotted the holdings.   10

---

4 **Hypereia**] This literally translates as 'Beyond-land', or 'the far away place'. Note that both the Cyclopes and the Phaiakians are descended from Poseidon, but display very different characteristics. The Cyclopes are wild and uncultivated, whereas the Phaiakians are perhaps excessively refined.

5 **overbearing**] Elsewhere in the *Odyssey*, this epithet is used only of the suitors.

8 **Scheria**] As with many places in the *Odyssey*, there has been much debate as to which real place (if any) this corresponds to. Corfu (Corcyra) is the most frequent suggestion – though some have objected that this is too close to Ithaka. Samuel Butler thought that it was a town on Sicily and (as Jones points out, ad loc.), there is no reason to assume that it is an island.

8 **far away from men who eat bread**] This formula occurs frequently. See, for example, IX.89, and the Introduction to Book IX.

But now he had submitted to his fate, and gone to Hades,
and Alkinoös, learned in designs from the gods, now ruled there.
It was to his house that the gray-eyed goddess Athene
went, devising the homecoming of great-hearted Odysseus,
as she went into the ornate chamber, in which a girl   15
was sleeping, like the immortal goddesses for stature and beauty,
Nausikaa, the daughter of great-hearted Alkinoös,
and beside her two handmaidens with beauty given from the Graces
slept on either side of the post with the shining doors closed.
She drifted in like a breath of wind to where the girl slept,   20
and came and stood above her head and spoke a word to her,
likening herself to the daughter of Dymas, famed for seafaring,
a girl of the same age, in whom her fancy delighted.
In this likeness the gray-eyed Athene* spoke to her:
'Nausikaa, how could your mother have a child so careless?   25
The shining* clothes are lying away uncared for, while your
marriage is not far off,* when you should be in your glory
for clothes to wear, and provide too for those who attend you.
It is from such things that a good reputation among people
springs up, giving pleasure to your father and the lady your mother.   30
So let us go on a washing tomorrow when dawns shows. I too
will go along with you* and help you, so you can have all
done most quickly, since you will not long stay unmarried.
For already you are being courted by all the best men
of the Phaiakians hereabouts, and you too are a Phaiakian.   35
So come, urge your famous father early in the morning
to harness the mules and wagon for you, and it shall carry
the sashes and dresses and shining coverlets for you. In this way
it will be so much more becoming than for you to go there
on foot, for the washing places are a long way from the city.'   40
   So the gray-eyed Athene spoke and went away from her
to Olympos, where the abode of the gods stands firm and unmoving
forever, they say, and so not shaken with winds nor spattered
with rains, nor does snow pile ever there, but the shining bright air
stretches cloudless away, and the white light glances upon it.   45
And there, and all their days, the blessed gods take their pleasure.

20–4 Athene is not impersonating Dymas' daughter in the same way that she impersonated Mentes in Book I. Instead she causes Nausikaa to have a dream, while standing 'above her head'.

26 **shining**] Here, as often in Homeric epic, the epithet indicates the ideal, rather than the actual, state of the thing described. The clothes are in fact dirty. Similarly, in the *Iliad*, beached ships are described as 'swift'.

27 **marriage is not far off**] The first of several hints at Nausikaa's readiness to marry. The possibility that she and Odysseus might form an alliance is never far from the surface.

31–2 **I too / will go along with you**] Dymas' daughter is not mentioned during the subsequent trip to the washing place, but Athene herself is.

There the Gray-eyed One went, when she had talked with the young
   girl.
And the next the Dawn came, throned in splendor, and wakened the
   well-robed
girl Nausikaa, and she wondered much at her dreaming,
and went through the house, so as to give the word to her parents,   50
to her dear father and mother. She found them within there;
the queen was sitting by the fireside with her attendant
women, turning sea-purple yarn on a distaff; her father
she met as he was going out the door to the council
of famed barons, where the proud Phaiakians used to summon him.   55
She stood very close up to her dear father and spoke to him:
'Daddy dear,* will you not have them harness me the wagon,
the high one with the good wheels, so that I can take the clothing
to the river and wash it? Now it is lying about, all dirty,
and you yourself, when you sit among the first men in council   60
and share their counsels, ought to have clean clothing about you;
and also, you have five dear sons who are grown in the palace,
two of them married, and the other three are sprightly bachelors,
and they are forever wanting clean fresh clothing, to wear it
when they go to dance, and it is my duty to think about all this.'   65
   So she spoke, but she was ashamed to speak of her joyful
marriage to her dear father, but he understood all and answered:
'I do not begrudge you the mules, child, nor anything
else. So go, and the serving men will harness the wagon,
the high one with the good wheels that has the carrying basket.'   70
   He spoke, and gave the order to the serving men. These obeyed,
and brought the mule wagon with good wheels outside and put it
together, and led the mules under the yoke and harnessed them,
and the girl brought the bright clothing out from the inner chamber
and laid it in the well-polished wagon. Meanwhile her mother   75
put in a box all manner of food, which would preserve strength,
and put many good things to eat with it, and poured out
wine in a goatskin bottle, and her daughter put that in a wagon.
She gave her limpid olive oil in a golden oil flask
for her and her attendant women to use for anointing.   80
Nausikaa took up the whip and the shining reins, then
whipped them into a start and the mules went noisily forward
and pulled without stint, carrying the girl and the clothing.
She was not alone. The rest, her handmaidens, walked on beside
   her.

57–65 Nausikaa attempts to conceal her true motives – namely, to prepare for her marriage – but
Alkinoös sees through her. On this passage see Griffin 1980b: 61–4.

Now when they had come to the delightful stream of the river,   85
where there was always a washing place, and plenty of glorious
water that ran through to wash what was ever so dirty,
there they unyoked the mules and set them free from the wagon,
and chased them out along the bank of the swirling river
to graze on the sweet river grass, while they from the wagon   90
lifted the wash in their hands and carried it to the black water,
and stamped on it in the basins, making a race and game of it
until they had washed and rinsed all dirt away, then spread it
out in line along the beach of the sea, where the water
of the sea had washed the most big pebbles up on the dry shore.   95
Then they themselves, after bathing and anointing themselves with
    olive oil,
ate their dinner all along by the banks of the river
and waited for the laundry to dry out in the sunshine.
But when she and her maids had taken their pleasure in eating,
they all threw off their veils for a game of ball, and among them   100
it was Nausikaa of the white arms who led in the dancing;
and as Artemis,* who showers arrows, moves on the mountains
either along Taÿgetos or on high-towering
Erymanthos, delighting in boars and deer in their running,
and along with her the nymphs, daughters of Zeus of the aegis,   105
range in the wilds and play, and the heart of Leto is gladdened,
for the head and the brows of Artemis are above all the others,
and she is easily marked among them, though all are lovely,
so this one shone among her handmaidens, a virgin unwedded.
    But now, when she was about ready once more to harness   110
the mules, and fold the splendid clothing, and start on the way
    home,
then the gray-eyed goddess Athene thought what to do next;*
how Odysseus should awake,* and see the well-favored young girl,
and she should be his guide to the city of the Phaiakians.
Now the princess threw the ball towards one handmaiden,   115
and missed the girl, and the ball went swirling into the water,
and they all cried out aloud, and noble Odysseus wakened
and sat up and began pondering in his heart and his spirit:

102–9 **Artemis**] The Greek goddess of hunting, and also (significantly) a 'virgin unwedded' –
ready to take violent action whenever her virginity is threatened. The comparison heightens the
tension; we know Nausikaa is shortly to be confronted by the naked Odysseus.

112–14 A typical piece of Homeric foreshadowing. Athene's plans for Odysseus and Nausikaa
serve as a synopsis of the ensuing action.

113–18 We have seen first Nausikaa and now Odysseus wake up. It is unusual for an episode in
an epic poem to begin with both its major characters asleep. The fact that the action can develop
to this extent without their active participation points to the level of divine interference. It was
Athene herself who put Odysseus to sleep at V.491–3.

'Ah me,* what are the people whose land I have come to this time,
and are they violent and savage, without justice,   120
or hospitable to strangers, with a godly mind? See now
how an outcry of young women echoes about me,
of nymphs, who keep the sudden and sheer high mountain places
and springs of the rivers and grass of the meadows, or am I truly
in the neighborhood of human people I can converse with?   125
But come now, I myself shall see what I can discover.'
    So speaking, great Odysseus came from under his thicket,
and from the dense foliage with his heavy hand he broke off
a leafy branch to cover his body and hide the male parts,
and went in the confidence of his strength, like some hill-kept lion,*   130
who advances, though he is rained on and blown by the wind, and
    both eyes
kindle; he goes out after cattle or sheep, or it may be
deer in the wilderness, and his belly is urgent upon him
to get inside of a close steading and go for the sheepflocks.
So Odysseus was ready to face young girls with well-ordered   135
hair, naked though he was, for the need was on him; and yet
he appeared terrifying to them, all crusted with dry spray,
and they scattered one way and another down the jutting beaches.
Only the daughter of Alkinoös stood fast, for Athene
put courage into her heart, and took the fear from her body,   140
and she stood her ground and faced him, and now Odysseus
    debated
whether to supplicate* the well-favored girl by clasping
her knees, or stand off where he was and in words of blandishment
ask if she would show him the city, and lend him clothing.
Then in the division of his heart this seemed best to him,   145
to stand well off and supplicate in words of blandishment,
for fear that if he clasped her knees, the girl might be angry.
So blandishingly and full of craft he began to address her:

119–21 These lines are repeated at XIII.200–2, when Odysseus awakes on the Ithakan shore, and 120–1 reappear at IX.175–6, when he goes to see the Cyclops.

130–5 **like some hill-kept lion . . . So Odysseus**] Odysseus went to sleep on the Scherian coast afraid that he might 'become spoil and prey to the wild animals' (V.473), but it is he who has ended up in the role of a wild beast. An almost identical simile occurs at *Iliad* XII.299–307, where it is used of the Trojan warrior Sarpedon advancing into battle. There, the lion is moved by his 'proud heart', here it is because 'his belly is urgent upon him'. The effect is a sort of parody – not of the specific simile but of the kind of Iliadic heroism from which Odysseus is now so far removed. Note that the needs of the belly are given particular prominence in the *Odyssey* (see further pp. 14–15).

141–2 **debated / whether to supplicate**] Proper supplication demands that physical contact is made – but Odysseus is naked, and the threat of rape overshadows the encounter, so he decides to keep his distance; see Gould (1973).

'I am at your knees,* O queen. But are you mortal or goddess?
If indeed you are one of the gods who hold wide heaven,   150
then I must find in you the nearest likeness to Artemis
the daughter of great Zeus, for beauty, figure, and stature.
But if you are one among the mortals who live in this country,
three times blessed are your father and the lady your mother,
and three times blessed are your brothers too, and I know their spirits   155
are warmed forever with happiness at the thought of you, seeing
such a slip of beauty taking her place in the chorus of dancers;
but blessed at the heart, even beyond these others, is that one
who, after loading you down with gifts, leads you as his bride
home. I have never with these eyes seen anything like you,   160
neither man nor woman. Wonder takes me as I look on you.
Yet in Delos* once I saw such a thing, by Apollo's altar.
I saw the stalk of a young palm shooting up. I had gone there
once, and with a following of a great many people,
on that journey which was to mean hard suffering for me.   165
And as, when I looked upon that tree, my heart admired it
long, since such a tree had never sprung from the earth, so
now, lady, I admire you and wonder, and am terribly
afraid to clasp you by the knees.* The hard sorrow is on me.
Yesterday on the twentieth day I escaped the wine-blue   170
sea; until then the current and the tearing winds had swept me
along from the island Ogygia,* and my fate has landed me
here; here too I must have evil to suffer; I do not
think it will stop; before then the gods have much to give me.
Then have pity, O queen. You are the first I have come to   175
after much suffering, there is no one else that I know of
here among the people who hold this land and this city.
Show me the way to the town and give me some rag to wrap me
in, if you had any kind of piece of cloth when you came here,
and then may the gods give you everything that your heart longs for;   180
may they grant you a husband* and a house and sweet agreement
in all things, for nothing is better than this, more steadfast
than when two people, a man and his wife, keep a harmonious

---

149 **I am at your knees**] Odysseus' words translate literally as, 'I grasp your knees.' Although he has decided to keep his distance, the language of formal supplication lingers.

162 **Delos**] The island on which Leto gave birth to her twins, Apollo and Artemis. Odysseus travelled there with Menelaos before the Trojan expedition, in order to ask King Anius if his daughters would accompany the Greek army (Graves 1960: 160.u; the story is not in Homer). The mention of a large retinue stresses his former importance.

168–9 **terribly / afraid to grasp you by the knees**] Odysseus suggests that it is Nausikaa's beauty, rather than his own nakedness, that makes him unable to supplicate her formally.

172 **Ogygia**] Kalypso's island.

181–5 The blessing reminds the audience of Odysseus' marriage to Penelope, and hints (again) at the possibility that Nausikaa and Odysseus will marry.

household; a thing that brings much distress to the people who hate
    them
and pleasure to their well-wishers, and for them the best reputation.' 185
    Then in turn Nausikaa of the white arms answered him:
'My friend,* since you seem not like a thoughtless man, nor a mean
    one,
it is Zeus himself, the Olympian, who gives people good fortune,
to each single man, to the good and the bad, just as he wishes;
and since he must have given you yours, you must even endure it. 190
But now, since it is our land and our city that you have come to,
you shall not lack for clothing nor anything else, of those gifts
which should befall the unhappy suppliant on his arrival;
and I will show you our town, and tell you the name of our people.
It is the Phaiakians who hold this territory and city, 195
and I myself am the daughter of great-hearted Alkinoös,
whose power and dominion are held by right, given from the
    Phaiakians.'
    She spoke, and to her attendants with well-ordered hair gave
      instruction:
'Stand fast, girls. Where are you flying, just because you have looked
    on
a man? Do you think this is some enemy coming against us? 200
There is no such man living nor can there ever be one
who can come into the land of the Phaiakians bringing
warlike attack; we are so very dear to the immortals,
and we live far apart by ourselves in the wash of the great sea
at the utter end, nor do any other people mix with us. 205
But, since this is some poor wanderer who has come to us,
we must now take care of him, since all strangers and wanderers
are sacred in the sight of Zeus, and the gift is a light and dear one.
So, my attendants, give some food and drink to the stranger,
and bathe him, where there is shelter from the wind, in the river.' 210
    She spoke, and they stopped their flight, encouraging each other,
and led Odysseus down to the sheltered place, as Nausikaa
daughter of great-hearted Alkinoös had told them
to do, and laid out for him to wear a mantle and tunic,
and gave him limpid olive oil in a golden oil flask, 215
and told him he could bathe himself* in the stream of the river.
Then the glorious Odysseus spoke to these serving maids:
'Stand as you are, girls, a little away from me, so that
I can wash the salt off my shoulders and use the olive oil

187–97 Nausikaa accepts Odysseus' supplication.
  216 **he could bathe himself**] Men are frequently bathed by servant-girls in Homer, so Odysseus'
reluctance to appear naked in front of them is odd.

on them. It is long since my skin has known any ointment.   220
but I will not bathe in front of you, for I feel embarrassed
in the presence of lovely-haired girls to appear all naked.'
   He spoke, and they went away and told it to their young mistress.
But when great Odysseus had bathed in the river and washed from
   his body
the salt brine, which clung to his back and his broad shoulders,   225
he scraped from his head the scurf of brine from the barren salt sea.
But when he had bathed all, and anointed himself with olive oil,
and put on the clothing this unwedded girl had given him,
then Athene, daughter of Zeus, made him seem taller*
for the eye to behold, and thicker, and on his head she arranged   230
the curling locks that hung down like hyacinthine petals.*
And as when a master craftsmen overlays gold on silver,
and he is one who was taught by Hephaistos* and Pallas Athene
in art complete, and grace is on every work he finishes,
so Athene gilded with grace his head and shoulders,   235
and he went a little aside and sat by himself on the seashore,
radiant in grace and good looks; and the girl admired him.
It was to her attendants with well-ordered hair that she now spoke:
'Hear me, my white-armed serving women; let me say something.
It is not against the will of all the gods on Olympos   240
that this man is here to be made known to the godlike Phaiakians.
A while ago he seemed an unpromising man to me. Now
he even resembles one of the gods, who hold high heaven.
If only the man to be called my husband could be like this one,
a man living here, if only this one were pleased to stay here.   245
But come, my attendants, give some food and drink to the stranger.'
   So she spoke, and they listened well to her and obeyed her,
and they set food and drink down beside Odysseus. He then,
noble and long-suffering Odysseus, eagerly
ate and drank, since he had not tasted food for a long time.   250
   Then Nausikaa of the white arms thought what to do next.
She folded the laundry and put it away in the fine mule wagon,
and yoked the mules with powerful hooves, and herself mounted,
and urged Odysseus and spoke a word and named him by title:
'Rise up now, stranger, to go to the city, so I can see you   255

229 **made him seem taller**] Odysseus is a short man; see p. 16 above.

231 **like hyacinthine petals**] Odysseus is imagined to have hair hanging down in tight curls, and the simile captures this beautifully. The unusual word (Gk *huakinthinos*) is picked up in *Paradise Lost*, when Milton describes how Adam's 'hyacinthe locks / Round from his parted forelock manly hung / Clustering' (IV.300–2). The allusion is a pointed one: Adam's innocent nakedness before the fall is made to resemble Odysseus' threatening appearance on the coast of Scheria.

233 **Hephaistos**] The god of fire, and associated with craftsmanship. See XXIII 159–62, where the simile is repeated.

to the house of my own prudent father, where I am confident
you will be made known to all the highest Phaiakians.
Or rather, do it this way; you seem to me not to be thoughtless.
While we are still among the fields and the lands that the people
work, for that time follow the mules and the wagon, walking   260
lightly along with the maids, and I will point the way to you.
But when we come to the city, and around this is a towering
wall, and a handsome harbor either side of the city,
and a narrow causeway, and along the road there are oarswept
ships drawn up, for they all have slips, one for each vessel;   265
and there is a place of assembly, put together with quarried
stone, and built around a fine precinct of Poseidon,
and there they tend to all that gear that goes with the black ships,
the hawsers and the sails, and there they fine down their oarblades;
for the Phaiakians have no concern with the bow or the quiver,   270
but it is all masts and the oars of ships and the balanced vessels
themselves, in which they delight in crossing over the gray sea;
and it is their graceless speech I shrink from, for fear one may mock
   us
hereafter, since there are insolent men* in our community,
and see how one of the worse sort might say when he met us,   275
"Who is this large and handsome stranger whom Nausikaa
has with her, and where did she find him? Surely, he is
to be her husband, but is he a stray from some ship of alien
men she found for herself, since there are no such hereabouts?
Or did some god after much entreaty come down in answer   280
to her prayers, out of the sky, and all his days will he have her?
Better so, if she goes out herself and finds her a husband
from elsewhere, since she pays no heed to her own Phaiakian
neighbors, although many of these and the best ones court her."
So they will speak, and that would be a scandal against me,   285
and I myself would disapprove of a girl who acted
so, that is, without the good will of her dear father
and mother making friends with a man,* before being formally
married. Then, stranger, understand what I say, in order
soon to win escort and a voyage home* from my father.   290
You will find a glorious grove of poplars sacred to Athene
near the road, and a spring runs there, and there is a meadow

---

274 **insolent men**] A reminder of the situation in Ithaka, where Penelope is also troubled by men
who are insolent (Gk *huperphialos*), an epithet regularly used of the suitors.

288 **making friends with a man**] The Greek word for 'mingle' or 'make friends' (*misgetai*) can
also be used as a euphemism for 'have sex'.

290 **a voyage home**] Odysseus has not yet mentioned his desire to return home, but Nausikaa
assumes that this is his aim. The assumption sits awkwardly with the frequent references to
marriage.

about it, and there is my father's estate and his flowering orchard,
as far from the city as the shout of a man will carry.
Sit down there and wait for time enough for the rest of us   295
to reach the town and make our way to my father's palace.
But when you estimate that we shall have reached the palace,
then go to the city of the Phaiakians and inquire for
the palace of my father, great-hearted Alkinoös. This is
easily distinguished, so an innocent child could guide you*   300
there, for there are no other houses built for the other
Phaiakians anything like the house of the hero Alkinoös.
But when you have disappeared inside the house and the courtyard,
then go on quickly across the hall until you come to
my mother, and she will be sitting beside the hearth, in the firelight,   305
turning sea-purple yarn on a distaff, a wonder to look at,
and leaning against the pillar, and her maids are sitting behind her;
and there is my father's chair of state, drawn close beside her,
on which he sits when he drinks his wine like any immortal.
Go on past him and then with your arms embrace our mother's   310
knees; do this, so as to behold your day of homecoming
with happiness and speed, even if you live very far off.
For if she has thoughts in her mind that are friendly to you,
then there is hope that you can see your own people, and come back
to your strong-founded house, and to the land of your fathers.'   315
   So Nausikaa spoke and with shining lash whipped up
her mules, and swiftly they left the running river behind them,
and the mules, neatly twinkling their feet, ran very strongly,
but she drove them with care, so that those on foot, Odysseus
and the serving maids, could keep up, and used the whip with
   discretion.   320
And the sun went down and they came to the famous grove, sacred
to Athene; and there the great Odysseus sat down
and immediately thereafter prayed to the daughter of great Zeus:
'Hear me, Atrytone* child of Zeus of the aegis,
and listen to me now, since before you did not listen   325
to my stricken voice as the famous shaker of the earth* battered me.
Grant that I come, as one loved and pitied, among the Phaiakians.'
   So he spoke in prayer, and Pallas Athene heard him,
but she did not yet show herself before him, for she respected
her father's brother, Poseidon, who still nursed a sore anger   330
at godlike Odysseus until his arrival in his own country.

---

300 **an innocent child could guide you**] Odysseus will in fact be guided by Athene.
324 **Atrytone**] A cult title of Athene. It means 'unwearying'.
326 **the famous shaker of the earth**] Poseidon.

Book IX: Odysseus as Storyteller: Polyphemos

Odysseus has been fed and now, in accordance with the laws of guest-friendship (see p. 23 above), it is time for him to reveal his identity. He does so in a striking way:

> I am Odysseus son of Laertes, known before all men
> for the study of crafty designs [*doloisin*], and my fame goes up to the
>   heavens.

Many translators have shied away from an honest translation of *doloisin* (cunning, trickery, deceit). Alexander Pope rendered it as 'wisdom', and justified the decision in a lengthy footnote. Rieu translated it as 'strategems'. Lattimore's 'the study of crafty designs' is more accurate than most (though it is wooden, and makes Odysseus seem strangely professorial). Odysseus' most famous act of deceit was of course his construction of the Wooden Horse (referred to at VIII.500–20), but the story he is about to tell the Phaiakian court is also concerned with his guile: the tricking and blinding of Polyphemos. Odysseus will tell the Phaiakians how he outwitted the Cyclops, 'combining all my resources and treacheries, / as with life at stake, for the great evil was very close to us' (IX.422–3). Odysseus plainly regards the dire situation he was in as justification for his deceitful actions (though some readers have dissented), but it is problematic for him to be advertising his propensity for cunning in front of a group of strangers. Indeed, a question mark has always hung over the truthfulness of Odysseus' narration (which occupies most of the next four books of the poem). Alkinoös pays him a dry and double-edged compliment when he observes that Odysseus has told his story 'expertly, as a singer would do' (XI.368). Granted, he also stresses that he and his court do not regard their guest as one of those 'people who wander widely, making up / lying stories, from which no one could learn anything' – but once readers have considered the possibility that Odysseus is lying it is hard for them to dispel their doubts. Might we regard the whole of Books IX to XII as merely the largest of the 'lying tales' for which Odysseus is renowned? (See Goldhill 1991: 24–68, and on Book XIII below) From a technical point of view, the narration incorporates bits and pieces of various folk tales – and the joins are more clearly visible here than almost anywhere else in the Homeric poems (see Page 1955). Another critic has suggested that there might be a practical function of Odysseus' narration, and that he tailors the details of his narrative to fit his audience: he tells the story of a monster who refuses to obey the laws of hospitality, and of two women who seek to detain him – in order, perhaps, that Alkinoös avoids the example of Polyphemos, and Nausikaa avoids the example of Circe and Kalypso (Most 1989).

Irrespective of its accuracy, Odysseus' account is important in stressing his own values, as an Ithakan and as a Greek. Throughout his travels, he places huge importance on the notion of *hiketeia*, or supplication (see Book VI above), and the failure of supplication in the Cyclops' cave only serves to remind us of the value system that works so well elsewhere – as, for example, on the Scherian coast, where Nausikaa has accepted Odysseus' supplication. As one critic has put it, 'supplicating Polyphemus is like offering a Martian a cup of tea: a touchingly stupid act by someone who is sure that the rituals for greeting strangers work their magic in all areas' (Burrow 1993: 26). Odysseus' cultural assumptions are also revealed by the formula with which he describes the unknown peoples he is about to encounter at the start of his journey: 'eaters of bread' (IX.89). But while Odysseus expects them to eat conventional food – of the sort found in Ithaka – these people eat the lotus-fruit, a substance which causes them to forget their homeland, a place rooted in agriculture. Odysseus first describes Polyphemos not as a monster but as a man (Gk *anēr*, l. 187), but soon adjusts his opinion: 'he was a monstrous wonder made to behold, not / like a man, an eater of bread' (190–1). We are never told whether Polyphemos actually eats bread – but it is crucial that neither he nor the other Cyclopes participate in the agricultural practices by which the Ithakans define themselves. He herds goats in the fashion of a character from a bucolic poem, but his island is plainly susceptible to more intensive cultivation, as Odysseus – speaking like a true colonist – observes:

> For it is not a bad place at all, it could bear all crops
> in season, and there are meadow lands near the shores of the gray
>   sea,
> well-watered and soft; there could be grapes grown endlessly,
> and there is smooth land for plowing, men could reap a full harvest
> always in season, since there is a very rich subsoil. (131–5)

It is the Cyclops' failure to exploit this landscape which excludes him from the ranks of the breadeaters (Gk *sitophagoi*). As Pierre Vidal-Naquet puts it in his essay on cultivation in the *Odyssey*, 'the real point is that the counterpart of the age of gold is the age of cannibalism' (1996: 41).

From this point of view, it is hardly surprising that the outwitting of the Cyclops has often been Odysseus' most highly praised action

– allegorised as the triumph of reason over man's baser nature. Pope approvingly records Eustathius' view of Polyphemos' single eye: 'in anger, or any violent passion, men see but one single object as that passion directs, or see but with one eye . . . and that passion transforms us into a kind of savages, and makes us brutal and sanguinary, like this *Polyphemus*' (Pope 1967: IX.309). Interpretations of this sort abound – and, needless to say, Polyphemos' restricted (and ultimately obliterated) vision is frequently played on. Following the execution of Charles I in 1649, royalists often compared the kingless commonwealth to the blinded Polyphemos. John Dryden, as he celebrated the Restoration of the monarchy in 1660, wrote of the parliamentary faction that 'Blind as the Cyclops, and as wild as he, / They owned a lawless, salvage liberty' (*Astraea Redux*, ll. 45–6). The philosopher John Locke used the encounter between Odysseus and Polyphemos to demonstrate that there are moments when violence is necessary, pouring scorn on those who suggested that rebellion was never justified by pointing to the Ithakans' predicament when trapped in the cave: 'And no doubt *Ulysses*, who was a prudent Man, preach'd up Passive Obedience, and exhorted them to a quiet Submission, by representing to them of what concernment Peace was to Mankind' (Locke 1988: 417). And Immanuel Kant invoked the figure of the Cyclops in order to describe a kind of philosophical tunnel vision that ran counter to the values of the Enlightenment (see Hall 2008: 93).

There is, though, another recurrent interpretation of the episode, discussed at length by Hall (93–100). If Odysseus' defeat of the Cyclops is an emblem of Greek hegemony – and of colonialism more generally – then it is understandable that it has come under close scrutiny over the past century. Theodor Adorno and Max Horkheimer, in their influential *Dialectic of Enlightenment* (1944) used the encounter as a parable for the interaction between 'reason' and 'nature'. For them, Odysseus is a 'bearer of culture', who cynically manipulates the Cyclops' underdeveloped intellect: 'The giant's stupidity, the basis of his barbaric brutality as long as his cause prospers, represents something better once it is overthrown by one who should know better.' (Adorno and Horkheimer 2002: 52) Writers approaching the episode from a post-colonial perspective have also had sympathy for Polyphemos (on which, see Wynter 2002). One can, after all, regard Polyphemos' freedom as more than mere liberty from reason. He is, from one point of view, a quiet, pastoral figure, who tends his flocks and makes cheeses – until he returns to his cave one day, and finds twelve men helping themselves to his food. He appears in the poem as a drunken, man-eating monster, but before

Odysseus landed on his island he was teetotal and vegetarian. There is at least a disturbing similarity between the effect that contact with outsiders has on Polyphemus and the effects it has had on various 'discovered' and colonised groups around the world.

> Then resourceful Odysseus spoke in turn and answered him:
> 'O great Alkinoös, pre-eminent among all people,
> surely indeed it is a good thing to listen to a singer
> such as this one* before us, who is like the gods in his singing;
> for I think there is no occasion accomplished that is more pleasant   5
> than when festivity holds sway among all the populace,
> and the feasters up and down the houses are sitting in order
> and listening to the singer, and beside them the tables are loaded
> with bread and meats, and from the mixing bowl the wine steward
> draws the wine and carries it about and fills the cups. This   10
> seems to my own mind to be the best of occasions.
> But now your wish was inclined to ask me about my mournful
> sufferings, so that I must mourn and grieve even more. What then
> shall I recite to you first of all, what leave till later?
> Many are the sorrows the gods of the sky have given me.   15
> Now first I will tell you my name,* so that all of you
> may know me, and I hereafter, escaping the day without pity,
> be your friend and guest, though the home where I live is far away
>   from you.
> I am Odysseus son of Laertes, known before all men
> for the study of crafty designs, and my fame goes up to the heavens.   20
> I am at home in sunny Ithaka. There is a mountain
> there that stands tall, leaf-trembling Neritos, and there are islands
> settled around it, lying one very close to another.
> There is Doulichion and Same, wooded Zakynthos,
> but my island lies low and away,* last of all on the water   25
> toward the dark, with the rest below facing east and sunshine,
> a rugged place, but a good nurse of men; for my part
> I cannot think of any place sweeter on the earth to look at.

4 **such as this one**] Demodokos, the bard of the Phaiakians. In Book VIII he sang of the fall of Troy, causing Odysseus to weep – and Alkinoös to press the mysterious guest as to his true identity.

16 **Now first I will tell you my name**] At the close of Book VIII, Alkinoös had asked Odysseus four questions: 'What is your name?', 'Where do you come from?', 'What lands have you visited?' and 'Why are you crying?' The first two questions are dealt with in the first forty lines of Book IX; the rest of Books IX–XII addresses the second two questions. The laws of guest-friendship require Odysseus to reveal his name, but only after he has been welcomed and fed.

25 **my island lies low and away**] The meaning of these lines has been endlessly scrutinised by readers keen to discover the 'true' identity of Odysseus' island. But, as Heubeck writes (1989: 14), such investigations are likely to be fruitless: 'the poet cannot have been writing on the basis of first-hand knowledge, or even with map in hand'.

For in truth Kalypso, shining among divinities, kept me
with her in her hollow caverns, desiring me for her husband,   30
and so likewise Aiaian Circe the guileful detained me
beside her in her halls, desiring me for her husband,
but never could she persuade the heart within me. So it is
that nothing is more sweet in the end than country and parents
ever, even when far away one lives in a fertile   35
place, when it is an alien country, far from his parents.
But come, I will tell you of my voyage home with its many
troubles, which Zeus inflicted on me as I came home from Troy
    land.
    'From Ilion the wind took me and drove me ashore at Ismaros
by the Kikonians.* I sacked their city* and killed their people,   40
and out of their city taking their wives and many possessions
we shared them out, so none might go cheated of his proper
portion. There I was for the light foot and escaping,
and urged it, but they were greatly foolish and would not listen,
and then and there much wine was being drunk,* and they slaughtered
    many   45
sheep on the beach, and lumbering horn-curved cattle.
But meanwhile the Kikonians went and summoned the other
Kikonians, who were their neighbors living in the inland country,
more numerous and better men, well skilled in fighting
men with horses, but knowing too at need the battle   50
on foot. They came at early morning, like flowers in season*
or leaves, and the luck that came our way from Zeus was evil,
to make us unfortunate, so we must have hard pains to suffer.
Both sides stood and fought their battle there by the running
ships, and with bronze-headed spears they cast at each other,   55
and as long as it was early and the sacred daylight increasing,
so long we stood fast and fought them off, though there were more
    of them;
but when the sun had gone to the time for unyoking of cattle,
then at last the Kikonians turned the Achaians back and beat them,
and out of each ship six of my strong-greaved companions   60

39–40 **at Ismaros / by the Kikonians**] The Kikonians are mentioned at *Iliad* II.846, as allies of
the Trojans. Ismaros is in Thrace.

40–6 **I sacked their city**] The passage shows Odysseus and his men in a bad light, drunken and
murderous. In Book III we have heard Menelaos describe the more peaceful means by which he
acquired possessions during his return from Troy.

45 **much wine was being drunk**] Wine plays an important role in Book IX. We later discover (at
197–200) that this Kikonian wine was given to Odysseus by a priest of Apollo.

51–2 **like flowers in season**] An astonishingly tender point of comparison for people whose
sole aim is to kill. Compare *Iliad* II.469–70 (of the Achaian forces): 'They took position in the
blossoming meadow of Skamandros, / thousands of them, as leaves and flowers appear in season'

were killed,* but the rest of us fled away from death and
   destruction.
'From there we sailed on further along, glad to have escaped death,
but grieving still at heart for the loss of our dear companions.
Even then I would not suffer the flight of my oarswept vessels
until a cry had been made three times for each of my wretched   65
companions, who died there in the plain, killed by the Kikonians.
Cloud-gathering Zeus drove the North Wind against our vessels
in a supernatural storm, and huddled under the cloud scuds
land alike and the great water. Night sprang from heaven.
The ships were swept along yawning down the current; the
   violence   70
of the wind ripped our sails into three and four pieces. These then,
in fear of destruction, we took down and stowed in the ships' hulls,
and rowed them on ourselves until we had made the mainland.
There for two nights and two days together we lay up,
for pain and weariness together eating our hearts out.   75
But when the fair-haired Dawn in her rounds brought on the third
   day,
we, setting the masts upright, and hoisting the white sails on them,
sat still, and let the wind and the steersmen hold them steady.
And now I would have come home unscathed to the land of my
   fathers,
but as I turned the hook of Maleia,* the sea and current   80
and the North Wind beat me off course, and drove me on past
   Kythera.*
'Nine days then I was swept along by the force of the hostile
winds on the fishy sea, but on the tenth day we landed
in the country of the Lotus-Eaters, who live on a flowering
food, and there we set foot on the mainland, and fetched water,   85
and my companions took their supper there by the fast ships.
But after we had tasted of food and drink, then I sent
some of my companions ahead, telling them to find out
what men, eaters of bread, might live here* in this country.
I chose two men, and sent a third with them, as herald.   90

60–1 Odysseus left Troy with twelve ships, so lost 72 men in total. Six is a standard number
for losses in Odysseus' account. He loses six men to Skylla at XII.245, Circe having predicted this
at XII.110.

80 **Maleia**] The southernmost point of the Peloponnese.

81 **Kythera**] An island off the southern tip of Greece. From now on, none of the place names
given in Odysseus' account correspond to real places.

89 **what men, eaters of bread, might live here**] This is a standard formula, which reveals
Odysseus' preconceptions. He assumes that the inhabitants of this country will share the agricultural and eating practices of the Ithakans – in fact their food will erase all memory of these
practices. The phrase is repeated at X.101; on this occasion, the inhabitants (the Laistrygones)
turn out to be cannibals.

My men went on and presently met the Lotus-Eaters,
nor did these Lotus-Easters have any thoughts of destroying
our companions, but they only gave them lotus to taste of.
But any of them who ate the honey-sweet fruit of lotus
was unwilling to take any message back, or to go   95
away, but they wanted to stay there with the lotus-eating
people, feeding on lotus, and forget the way home. I myself
took these men back weeping, by force, to where the ships were,
and put them aboard under the rowing benches and tied them
fast, then gave the order to the rest of my eager   100
companions to embark on the ships in haste, for fear
someone else might taste of the lotus and forget the way home,
and the men quickly went aboard and sat to the oarlocks,
and sitting well in order dashed the oars in the gray sea.
  'From there, grieving still at heart, we sailed on further   105
along, and reached the country of the lawless outrageous
Cyclopes who, putting all their trust in the immortal
gods, neither plow with their hands nor plant anything,*
but all grows for them without seed planting, without cultivation,
wheat and barley and also the grapevines, which yield for them   110
wine of strength,* and it is Zeus' rain that waters it for them.
There people have no institutions, no meetings for counsels;
rather they make their habitation in caverns hollowed
among the peaks of the high mountains, and each one is the law
for his own wives and children, and cares nothing about the others.   115
  'There is a wooded island that spreads, away from the harbor,*
neither close in to the land of the Cyclopes nor far off
from it; forested; wild goats beyond number breed there,
for there is no coming and going of human kind to disturb them,
nor are they visited by hunters, who in the forest   120
suffer hardships as they haunt the peaks of the mountains,
neither again is it held by herded flocks, nor farmers,
but all its days, never plowed up and never planted,
it goes without people and supports the bleating wild goats.
For the Cyclopes have no ships* with cheeks of vermilion,   125
nor have they builders of ships among them, who could have made
  them

---

108 neither plow . . . nor plant anything] The Cyclopes' idyllic lifestyle corresponds to ancient
accounts of the golden age. See Hesiod 1964: *Works and Days*, 117–18
  110–11 which yield for them/ wine of strength] Polyphemos has never tasted wine, and the
description is therefore misleading.
  116–41 All this description is retrospective; Odysseus arrives under cover of darkness.
  125 no ships] This is another consistent feature of idyllic, primitive societies – as described in
ancient literature. It is also worth bearing in mind that Odysseus is addressing the Phaiakians, to
whose existence ships are central.

strong-benched vessels, and these if made could have run them
    sailings
to all the various cities of men, in the way that people
cross the sea by means of ships and visit each other,
and they could have made this island a strong settlement for them.   130
For it is not a bad place at all,* it could bear all crops
in season, and there are meadow lands near the shores of the gray
    sea,
well watered and soft; there could be grapes grown there endlessly,
and there is smooth land for plowing, men could reap a full harvest
always in season, since there is very rich subsoil. Also   135
there is an easy harbor, with no need for a hawser
nor anchor stone to be thrown ashore nor cables to make fast;
one could just run ashore and wait for the right time when the
    sailors'
desire stirred them to go and the right winds were blowing.
Also at the head of the harbor there runs bright water,   140
spring beneath rock, and there are black poplars growing around it.
There we sailed ashore, and there was some god* guiding
us in through the gloom of the night, nothing showed to look at,
for there was a deep mist around the ships, nor was there any moon
showing in the sky, but she was under the clouds and hidden.   145
There was none of us there whose eyes had spied out the island,
and we never saw any long waves rolling in and breaking
on the shore, but the first thing was when we beached the well-
    benched vessels.
Then after we had beached the ships we took all the sails down,
and we ourselves stepped out onto the break of the sea beach,   150
and there we fell asleep and waited for the divine Dawn.
    'But when the young Dawn showed again with her rosy fingers,*
we had a tour about the island, admiring everything
there, and the nymphs, daughters of Zeus of the aegis, started
the hill-roving goats our way for my companions to feast on.   155
At once we went and took from the ships curved bows and javelins
with long sockets, and arranging ourselves in three divisions
cast about, and the god granted us the game we longed for.
Now there were twelve ships that went with me, and for each one
    nine goats

131–5 The fertility of the Cyclopes' land is similar to that in Scheria (see VII.112–32).

142 **some god**] Here and at 158 Odysseus ascribes his good fortune to an unknown god – whose influence turns out to be malign.

151 **But when the young Dawn . . . fingers**] This stock phrase is repeated regularly (with slight variations) throughout the poem (at, e.g., IX.437); falling back on uniform descriptions of events such as sunrise was a useful device for the oral poet.

were portioned out, but I alone had ten for my portion.   160
So for the whole length of the day until the sun's setting,
we sat there feasting on unlimited meat and sweet wine;
for the red wine had not yet given out in the ships, there was
still some left, for we all had taken away a great deal
in storing jars* when we stormed the Kikonians' sacred citadel.   165
We looked across at the land of the Cyclopes, and they were
near by, and we saw their smoke and heard sheep and goats
    bleating.
But when the sun went down and the sacred darkness came over,
then we lay down to sleep along the break of the seashore;
but when the young Dawn showed again with her rosy fingers,   170
then I held an assembly and spoke forth before all:
"The rest of you, who are my eager companions, wait here,
while I with my own ship and companions that are in it,
go and find out about these people, and learn what they are,
whether they are savage and violent, and without justice,   175
or hospitable to strangers and with minds that are godly."
   'So speaking I went aboard the ship and told my companions
also to go aboard, and to cast off the stern cables,
and quickly they went aboard the ship and sat to the oarlocks,
and sitting well in order dashed the oars in the gray sea.   180
But when we had arrived at the place, which was nearby, there
at the end of the land we saw the cave, close to the water,
high, and overgrown with laurels, and in it were stabled
great flocks, sheep and goats alike, and there was a fenced yard
built around it with a high wall of grubbed-out boulders   185
and tall pines and oaks with lofty foliage. Inside
there lodged a monster of man, who now was herding
the flocks at a distance away, alone, for he did not range with
others, but stayed away by himself; his mind was lawless,
and in truth he was a monstrous wonder made to behold, not   190
like a man, an eater of bread,* but more like a wooded
peak of the high mountains seen standing away from the others.
   'At that time I told the rest of my eager companions
to stay where they were beside the ship and guard it. Meanwhile
I, choosing out the twelve best men among my companions,   195
went on, but I had with me a goatskin bottle of black wine,
sweet wine, given me by Maron, son of Euanthes
and priest of Apollo, who bestrides Ismaros; he gave it
because, respecting him with his wife and child, we saved them

---

164–5 **a great deal/ in storing jars**] The great quantity of the wine will be crucial in their encounter with Polyphemos.

190–1 **not/ like a man, an eater of bread**] Odysseus corrects the assumption he made at 89.

from harm. He made his dwelling among the trees of the sacred   200
grove of Phoibos Apollo, and he gave me glorious presents.
He gave me seven talents of well-wrought gold, and he gave me
a mixing bowl made all of silver, and gave along with it
wine, drawing it off in storing jars, twelve in all. This was
a sweet wine, unmixed, a divine drink. No one of his servants   205
or thralls that were in his household knew anything about it,
but only himself and his dear wife and a single housekeeper.
Whenever he drank this honey-sweet red wine, he would pour out
enough to full one cup, then twenty measures of water
were added,* and the mixing bowl gave off a sweet smell;   210
magical; then would be no pleasure in holding off. Of this
wine I filled a great wineskin full, and took too provisions
in a bag, for my proud heart had an idea* that presently
I would encounter a man who was endowed with great strength,
and wild, with no true knowledge of law or any good customs.   215
   'Lightly we made our way to the cave, but we did not find him
there, he was off herding on the range with his fat flocks.
We went inside the cave and admired everything inside it.
Baskets were there, heavy with cheeses, and the pens crowded
with lambs and kids. They had all been divided into separate   220
groups, the firstlings in one place, and then the middle ones,
the babies again by themselves. And all his vessels, milk pails
and pans, that he used for milking into, were running over
with whey. From the start my companions spoke to me and begged
      me
to take some of the cheeses, come back again, and the next time   225
to drive the lambs and kids from their pens, and get back quickly
to the ships again, and go sailing off across the salt water;
but I would not listen to them,* it would have been better their way,
not until I could see him, see if he would give me presents.*
My friends were to find the sight of him in no way lovely.*   230
   'There we built a fire and made sacrifice, and helping
ourselves to the cheese we ate and sat waiting for him
inside, until he came home from his herding. He carried a heavy

---

209–10 **twenty measures of water / were added**] Usually wine was diluted with two or three parts water. The Kikonian wine is very strong.

213–15 **my proud heart had an idea**] This would be astonishingly far-sighted. Is Odysseus altering the details of his adventure in order to impress his audience?

228 **I would not listen to them**] Odysseus admits his headstrong nature.

229 **presents**] The Greek word is *xeinia* – the gifts presented according to the laws of guest-friendship.

230 **in no way lovely**] As elsewhere in his account, Odysseus alternates between anticipating events that he is about to describe (as here) and suspending knowledge of them (as in the previous line).

load of dried-out wood, to make a fire for his dinner,
and threw it down inside the cave, making a terrible   235
crash, so in fear we scuttled away into the cave's corners.
Next he drove into the wide cavern all from the fat flocks
that he would milk, but he left all the male animals, billygoats
and rams, outside in his yard with the deep fences. Next thing,
he heaved up and set into position the huge door stop,   240
a massive thing; no twenty-two of the best four-wheeled
wagons could have taken that weight off the ground and carried it,
such a piece of sky-towering cliff that was he set over
his gateway. Next he sat down and milked his sheep and his bleating
goats, each of them in order, and put lamb or kid under each one   245
to suck, and then drew off half the white milk and put it
by in baskets made of wickerwork, stored for cheeses,
but let the other half stand in the milk pails so as to have it
to help himself to and drink from, and it would serve for his
    supper.
But after he had briskly done all his chores and finished,   250
at last he lit the fire and saw us and asked us a question:
'Strangers, who are you?* From where do you come sailing over the
    watery
ways? Is it on some business, or are you recklessly roving as pirates
    do,
when they sail on the salt sea and venture
their lives as they wander, bringing evil to alien people?"*   255
    'So he spoke, and the inward heart in us was broken
in terror of the deep voice and for seeing him so monstrous;
but even so I had words for an answer, and I said to him:
"We are Achaians coming from Troy, beaten off our true course
by winds from every direction across the great gulf of the open   260
sea, making for home, by the wrong way, on the wrong courses.
So we have come. So it has pleased Zeus to arrange it.
We claim we are of the following of the son of Atreus,
Agamemnon, whose fame now is the greatest thing under the heaven
such a city was that he sacked and destroyed so many   265
people; but now in turn we come to you and are suppliants
at your knees,* if you might give us a guest present or otherwise
some gift of grace, for such is the right of strangers. Therefore
respect the gods, O best of men. We are your suppliants,

---

252 **who are you?**] According to the laws of guest-friendship, hospitality should be offered
before the host asks the guest for his identity. Alkinoös only asks Odysseus his name at the start
of Book IX, for example. Crucially, Odysseus withholds his name from Polyphemos.
    255 **bringing evil to an alien people**] An accurate description of what is about to unfold.
    266-7 **suppliants/ at your knees**] See VI.141-2 and n.

and Zeus the guest god, who stands behind all strangers with
   honors   270
due them, avenges any wrong toward strangers and suppliants."
   'So I spoke, but he answered me in pitiless spirit:
"Stranger, you are a simple fool, or come from far off,
when you tell me to avoid the wrath of the gods or fear them.
The Cyclopes do not concern themselves over Zeus* of the aegis,   275
nor any of the rest of the blessed gods, since we are far better
than they, and for fear of the hate of Zeus I would not spare
you or your companions either, if the fancy took me
otherwise. But tell me, so I may know: where did you
put your well-made ship when you came? Nearby or far off?"   280
   'So he spoke, trying me out, but I knew too much and was not
deceived, but answered him in turn, and my words were crafty:*
"Poseidon, Shaker of the Earth, has shattered my vessel.
He drove it against the rocks on the outer coast of your country,
cracked on a cliff, it is done, the wind on the sea took it;   285
but I, with these you see, got away from sudden destruction."
   'So I spoke, but he in pitiless spirit answered
nothing, but sprang up and reached for my companions,
caught up two together and slapped them, like killing puppies,
against the ground, and the brains ran all over the floor, soaking   290
the ground. Then he cut them up limb by limb and got supper
   ready,
and like a lion reared in the hills, without leaving anything,*
ate them, entrails, flesh and the marrowy bones alike. We
cried out aloud and held our hands up to Zeus, seeing
the cruelty of what he did, but our hearts were helpless.   295
But when the Cyclops had filled his enormous stomach,
feeding on human flesh and drinking down milk unmixed* with
   water,
he lay down to sleep in the cave sprawled out through his sheep.
   Then I
took counsel with myself in my great-hearted spirit
to go up close, drawing from beside my thigh the sharp sword,   300
and stab him in the chest, where the midriff joins on the liver,

---

275–8 **The Cyclopes do not concern themselves over Zeus**] Compare Nausikaa's words to her attendants at VI.207–8: 'all strangers and wanderers / are sacred in the sight of Zeus'.

282 **my words were crafty**] Again, Odysseus takes pride in his capacity to deceive.

292 **without leaving anything**] When Homeric heroes eat, they first sacrifice an animal, and then set aside a portion for the gods. This is a sign of Polyphemos' impiety and lack of civilisation, as well as of his greed.

297 **unmixed**] An odd word to use of milk – it was no more usual to dilute it in the ancient world than it is now. The word glances forward to Polyphemos' wine drinking – and is perhaps a joke on Odysseus' part.

feeling for the place with my hand; but the second thought stayed
   me;*
for there we too would have perished away in sheer destruction,
seeing that our hands could never have pushed from the lofty
gate of the cave the ponderous boulder he had propped there.   305
So mourning we waited, just as we were, for the divine Dawn.
   'But when the young Dawn showed again with her rosy fingers,
he lit his fire, and then set about milking his glorious
flocks, each of them in order, and put lamb or kid under each one.
But after he had briskly done all his chores and finished,   310
again he snatched up two men, and prepared them for dinner,
and when he had dined, drove his fat flocks out of the cavern,
easily lifting off the great door stone, but then he put it
back again, like a man closing a lid on a quiver.*
And so the Cyclops, whistling loudly, guided his fat flocks   315
to the hills, leaving me there in the cave mumbling my black
   thoughts
of how I might punish him, how Athene might give me that glory.
And as I thought, this was the plan that seemed best to me.
The Cyclops had lying there beside the pen a great bludgeon
of olive wood, still green. He had cut it so that when it dried out   320
he could carry it about, and we looking at it considered
it to be about the size for the mast of a cargo-carrying
broad black ship of twenty oars which crosses the open
sea; such was the length of it, such the thickness, to judge by
looking. I went up and chopped a length of about a fathom,   325
and handed it over to my companions and told them to shave it
down, and they made it smooth, while I standing by them
   sharpened
the point, then put it over the blaze of the fire to harden.
Then I put it well away and hid it under the ordure
which was all over the floor of the cave, much stuff lying   330
about. Next I told the rest of the men to cast lots, to find out
which of them must endure with me to take up the great beam
and spin it in Cyclops' eye when sweet sleep had come over him.
The ones drew it whom I myself would have wanted chosen,
four men, and I myself was the fifth, and allotted with them.   335
With the evening he came back again, herding his fleecy
flocks, but drove all his fat flocks inside the wide cave

---

302 **the second thought stayed me**] Odysseus' initial plan – simply to kill the Cyclops – belongs in the world of the *Iliad*. In the *Odyssey* cunning is more useful than brute force.

  314 **like a man closing a lid on a quiver**] The ease with which Polyphemos shifts the doorstone looks forwards to the climactic moment when Odysseus strings his great bow, as easily as a bard strings a lyre (XXII.404–9).

at once, and did not leave any outside in the yard with the deep
   fence,
whether he had some idea, or whether a god so urged him.
When he had heaved up and set in position the huge door stop,   340
next he sat down and started milking his sheep and his bleating
goats, each of them in order, and put lamb or kid under each one.
But after he had briskly done all his chores and finished,
again he snatched up two men and prepared them for dinner.
Then at last I, holding in my hands an ivy bowl   345
full of the black wine,* stood close up to the Cyclops and spoke out:
"Here, Cyclops, have a drink of wine, now you have fed on
human flesh, and see what kind of drink our ship carried
inside her. I brought it for you, and it would have been your libation
had you taken pity and sent me home, but I cannot suffer   350
your rages. Cruel, how can any man come and visit
you ever again, now you have done what has no sanction?"
'So I spoke, and he took it and drank it off, and was terribly
pleased with the wine he drank and questioned me again, saying:
"Give me still more, freely, and tell me your name straightway   355
now, so I can give you a guest present to make you happy.
For the grain-giving land of the Cyclopes also yields them
wine of strength, and it is Zeus' rain that waters it for them;
but this comes from where ambrosia and nectar flow in abundance."
'So he spoke, and I gave him the gleaming wine again. Three times   360
I brought it to him and gave it to him, three times he recklessly
drained it, but when the wine had gone into the brains of the
   Cyclops,
then I spoke to him, and my words were full of beguilement:
"Cyclops, you ask me for my famous name. I will tell you
then, but you must give me a guest gift as you have promised.   365
Nobody is my name. My father and mother call me
Nobody, as do all the others who are my companions."
'So I spoke, and he answered me in pitiless spirit
"Then I will eat Nobody after his friends, and the others
I will eat first, and that shall be my guest present to you."   370
'He spoke and slumped away and fell on his back, and lay there
with his thick neck crooked over on one side, and sleep who
   subdues all
came on and captured him, and the wine gurgled up from his gullet
with gobs of human meat. This was his drunken vomiting.
Then I shoved the beam underneath a deep bed of cinders,   375
waiting for it to heat, and I spoke to all my companions

346 the black wine] That is, the wine described at IX.196–212 above.

in words of courage, so none should be in a panic, and back out;
but when the beam of olive, green as it was, was, nearly
at the point of catching fire and glowed, terribly incandescent,
then I brought it close up from the fire and my friends about me   380
stood fast. Some great divinity breathed courage into us.
They seized the beam of olive, sharp at the end, and leaned on it
into the eye, while I from above leaning my weight on it
twirled it, like man with a brace-and-bit who bores into
a ship timber, and his men from underneath, grasping   385
the strap on either side whirl it, and it bites resolutely deeper.
So seizing the fire-point-hardened timber we twirled it
in his eye, and the blood boiled around the hot point, so that
the blast and scorch of the burning ball singed all his eyebrows
and eyelids, and the fire made the roots of his eye crackle.   390
As when a man who works as a blacksmith plunges a screaming
great ax blade or plane into cold water, treating it
for temper, since this is the way steel is made strong, even
so Cyclops' eye sizzled about the beam of the olive.
He gave a giant horrible cry and the rocks rattled   395
to the sound, and we scuttled away in fear. He pulled the timber
out of his eye, and it blubbered with plenty of blood, then
when he had frantically taken it in his hands and thrown it
away, he cried aloud to the other Cyclopes, who live
around him in their own caves along the windy pinnacles.   400
They hearing him came swarming up from their various places,
and stood around the cave and asked him what was his trouble:
"Why, Polyphemos, what do you want with all this outcry
through the immortal night and have made us all thus sleepless?
Surely no mortal against your will can be driving your sheep off?   405
Surely none can be killing you by force or treachery?"
    'Then from inside the cave strong Polyphemos answered:
"Good friends, Nobody is killing me by force or treachery."
    'So then the others speaking in winged words gave him an answer:
"If alone as you are none uses violence on you,*   410
why, there is no avoiding the sickness sent by great Zeus;
so you had better pray to your father, the lord Poseidon."
    'So they spoke as they went away, and the heart within me
laughed over how my name and my perfect planning had fooled
    him.
But the Cyclops, groaning aloud and in the pain of his agony,   415
felt with his hands, and took the boulder out of the doorway,

*410 **none uses violence on you**] The Greek phrase meaning 'none' (*mē tis*) is very similar to the Greek word for 'deceit' or 'cunning' (*mētis*).

and sat down in the entrance himself, spreading his arms wide,
to catch anyone who tried to get out with the sheep, hoping
that I would be so guileless in my heart as to try this;
but I was planning so that things would come out the best way,   420
and trying to find some release from death, for my companions
and myself too, combining all my resources and treacheries,
as with life at stake, for the great evil was very close to us.
And as I thought, this was the plan that seemed best to me.
There were some male sheep, rams, well nourished, thick and fleecy,   425
handsome and large, with a dark depth of wool. Silently
I caught these and lashed them together with pliant willow
withes, where the monstrous Cyclops lawless of mind had used to
sleep. I had them in threes, and the one in the middle carried
a man, while the other two went on each side, so guarding   430
my friends. Three rams carried each man, but as for myself,
there was one ram, far the finest of all the flock. This one
I clasped around the back, snuggled under the wool of the belly,
and stayed there still, and with a firm twist of the hands and
    enduring
spirit clung fast to the glory of this fleece, unrelenting.   435
So we grieved for the last time and waited for the divine Dawn.
    'But when the young Dawn showed again with her rosy fingers,
then the male sheep hastened out of the case, toward pasture,
but the ewes were bleating all through the pens, unmilked, their
    udders
ready to burst. Meanwhile their master, suffering and in   440
bitter pain, felt over the backs of all his sheep, standing
up as they were, but in his guilelessness did not notice
how my men were fastened under the breasts of his fleecy
sheep. Last of all the flock the ram went out of the doorway,
loaded with his own fleece, and with me, and my close counsels.   445
Then, feeling him, powerful Polyphemos spoke a word to him:
"My dear old ram, why are you thus leaving the cave last of
the sheep?* Never in the old days were you left behind by
the flock, but long-striding, far ahead of the rest would pasture
on the tender bloom of the grass, be first at running rivers,   450
and be eager always to lead the way first back to the sheepfold
at evening. Now you are last of all. Perhaps you are grieving
for your master's eye, which a bad man and his wicked companions
put out, after he had made my brain helpless with wine, this
Nobody, who I think has not yet got clear of destruction.   455

447–60 In this affecting speech we see the events from Polyphemos' perspective for the first
time. He also shows himself to be capable of sympathy and affection – if only towards animals.

If only you could think like us and only be given
a voice, to tell me where he is skulking away from my anger,
then surely he would be smashed against the floor and his brains go
spattering all over the cave to make my heart lighter
from the burden of all the evils this niddering Nobody gave me.'   460
    'So he spoke, and sent the ram along from him, outdoors,
and when we had got a little way from the yard and the cavern,
first I got myself loose from my ram, then set my companions
free, and rapidly then, and with many a backward glance, we
drove the long-striding sheep, rich with fat, until we reached   465
our ship, and the sight of us who had escaped death was welcome
to our companions, but they began to mourn for the others;
only I would not let them cry out, but with my brows nodded
to each man, and told them to be quick and to load the fleecy
sheep on board* our vessel and sail out on the salt water.   470
Quickly they went aboard the ship and sat to the oarlocks,
and sitting well in order dashed the oars in the gray sea.
But when I was as far out from land as a voice shouting carries,
I called out aloud to the Cyclops, taunting him:
"Cyclops, in the end it was no weak man's companions   475
you were to eat by violence and force in your hollow
cave, and your evil deeds were to catch up with you, and be
too strong for you, hard one, who dared to eat your own guests
in your own house, so Zeus and the rest of the gods have punished
    you."*
    'So I spoke, and still more the heart in him was angered.   480
He broke away the peak of a great mountain and let it
fly, and threw it in front of the dark-prowed ship by only
a little, it just failed to graze the steering oar's edge,
but the sea washed up in the splash as the stone went under, the
    tidal
wave it made swept us suddenly back from the open   485
sea to the mainland again, and forced us on shore. Then I
caught up in my hands the very long pole and pushed her
clear again, and urged my companions with words, and nodding
with my head, to throw their weight on the oars and bring us
out of the threatening evil, and they leaned on and rowed hard.   490
But when we had cut through the sea to twice the previous distance,

---

469–70 **load the fleecy / sheep on board**] Odysseus had initially denied his men's request that
they steal the Cyclops' sheep.
    479 **Zeus and the rest of the gods have punished you**] Odysseus claims to be an agent of divine
justice; through him, Zeus punishes Polyphemos for violating the laws of hospitality. He makes
a similar claim about the fate of the suitors he kills, 'destroyed by the doom of the gods and their
own hard actions.' (XXII.413)

again I started to call to Cyclops, but my friends about me
checked me, first one and then another speaking, trying to soothe
   me:
"Hard one, why are you trying once more to stir up this savage
man, who just now threw his missile in the sea, forcing   495
our ship to the land again, and we thought once more we were
   finished;
and if he had heard a voice or any one of us speaking,
he would have broken all our heads and our ship's timbers
with a cast of a great jagged stone, so strong is his throwing."
   'So they spoke, but could not persuade the great heart in me,   500
but once again in the anger of my heart I cried to him:
"Cyclops, if any mortal man ever asks you who it was
that inflicted upon your eye this shameful blinding,
tell him that you were blinded by Odysseus,* sacker of cities.
Laertes is his father, and he makes his home in Ithaka."   505
   'So I spoke, and he groaned aloud and answered me, saying:
'Ah now, a prophecy spoken of old is come to completion.
There used to be a man here, great and strong, and a prophet,
Telemos, Eurymos' son, who for prophecy was pre-eminent
and grew old as a prophet among the Cyclopes. This man told me   510
how all this that has happened now must someday be accomplished,
and how I must lose the sight of my eye to the hands of Odysseus.
But always I was on the lookout for a man handsome
and tall, with great endowment of strength on him, to come here;
but now the end of it is that a little man, niddering, feeble,*   515
has taken away the sight of my eye, first making me helpless
with wine. So come here, Odysseus, let me give you a guest gift
and urge the glorious Shaker of the Earth to grant you conveyance
home. For I am his son, he announces himself as my father.
He himself will heal me, if he will, but not any other   520
one of the blessed gods, nor any man who is mortal."
   'So he spoke, but I answered him again and said to him:
"I only wish it were certain I could make you reft of spirit
and life, and send you to the house of Hades, as it is certain
that not even the Shaker of the Earth will ever heal your eye for you." 525
   'So I spoke, but he then called to the lord Poseidon
in prayer, reaching both arms up toward the starry heaven:

504 **you were blinded by Odysseus**] Having earlier told Polyphemos that he was punished
by Zeus, Odysseus now claims personal responsibility for his blinding. This is unwise, for two
reasons. First, his voice indicates his location to Polyphemos, who can continue to throw stones at
him. Second, by revealing his name, he enables Polyphemos to curse him.

515 **a little man, niddering, feeble**] The gap between Polyphemos' expectations and the reality
of Odysseus' physical stature reinforces the unusual nature of his heroism. He has defeated the
Cyclops by guile alone.

"Hear me, Poseidon who circle the earth, dark-haired. If truly
I am your son, and you acknowledge yourself as my father,
grant that Odysseus, sacker of cities, son of Laertes,   530
who makes his home in Ithaka, may never reach that home;
but if it is decided* that he shall see his own people,
and come home to his strong-founded house and to his own
    country,
let him come late, in bad case, with the loss of all his companions,
in someone else's ship, and find troubles in his household."   535
    'So he spoke in prayer, and the dark-haired god heard him.*
Then for the second time lifting a stone far greater
he whirled it and threw, leaning into the cast his strength beyond
    measure,
and the stone fell behind the dark-prowed ship by only
a little, it just failed to graze the steering oar's edge,   540
and the sea washed up in the splash as the stone went under; the
    tidal
wave drove us along forward and forced us onto the island.
But after we had so made the island, where the rest of
our strong-benched ships were waiting together, and our
    companions
were sitting about them grieving, having waited so long for us,   545
making this point we ran our ship on the sand and beached her,
and we ourselves stepped out onto the break of the sea beach,
and from the hollow ships bringing out the flocks of the Cyclops
we shared them out so none might go cheated of his proper
portion; but for me alone my strong-greaved companions   550
excepted the ram when the sheep were shared, and I sacrificed him
on the sands to Zeus,* dark-clouded son of Kronos, lord over
all, and burned him the thighs; but he was not moved by my
    offerings,*
but was still wondering on a way how all my strong-benched
ships should be destroyed and all my eager companions.   555
So for the whole length of the day until the sun's setting,
we sat there feasting on unlimited meat and sweet wine.

---

532 **but if it is decided**] Poseidon does not have the power to alter what has already been fated
– so Polyphemos adds a subclause to his curse.

536 **the dark-haired god heard him**] Polyphemos' curse is thus the ultimate source of Odysseus'
woes. See I.68–9.

551–2 **sacrificed him / on the sands to Zeus**] An important assertion of identity, having escaped
from a land where Greek cultural practices such as sacrifice and hospitality are held in contempt.
But Zeus rejects the sacrifice.

553 **he was not moved by my offerings**] Odysseus feels that Zeus is persecuting him, as well
as Poseidon – but there is no evidence for this in the rest of the poem. The only time when Zeus
directly hampers his homeward journey is when Odysseus' men have slaughtered Helios' cattle
(XII.374–419).

> But when the sun went down and the sacred darkness came over,
> then we lay down to sleep along the break of the seashore;
> but when the young Dawn showed again with her rosy fingers,   560
> then I urged on the rest of my companions and told them
> to go aboard their ships and to cast off the stern cables,
> and quickly they went aboard the ships and sat to the oarlocks,
> and sitting well in order dashed their oars in the gray sea.
> From there we sailed on further along, glad to have escaped death,   565
> but grieving still at heart for the loss of our dear companions.

Book XIII: Return to Ithaka

'Odyssey' has become a synonym for 'arduous journey' – but the second half of the poem is set almost entirely within Ithaka. Book XIII brings the hero fully out of the fairytale world of the poem's first half – the Phaiakian interlude acting as a kind of transitional phase – and lands him back on his native soil. But Athene has covered Ithaka with a mist, and Odysseus does not at first recognise his homeland, repeating the words he has previously used on arrival in Scheria (VI.119–21):

> 'Ah me, what are the people whose land I have come to this time,
> and are they savage and violent, and without justice,
> or hospitable to strangers and with minds that are godly? . . . '
>   (XIII.200–2)

One effect of this is plainly ironic; Athene has tricked Odysseus, and enjoys watching him as 'he in great sorrow / crept over the beach of his own country' (219–20). But the initial strangeness of Ithaka also provides both Odysseus and the reader with a warning of the dangers and deceptions to come.

The strange and indeterminate fate of the Phaiakian mariners is the last of the poem's other-worldly events. Our manuscripts of the poem may be faulty at this point (see commentary on line 158), which makes it still harder to work out what befalls them. It seems likely that the poet aimed for this uncertainty, since we cut away from Phaiakia for the last time at the critical moment. What is beyond doubt is that the Phaiakians are punished by Poseidon for showing excessive hospitality towards his enemy, Odysseus. This is perhaps surprising, given the constant emphasis on *xeinoi* having the favour and protection of Zeus; nowhere in the poem do we have such a clear view of the disagreement between gods (or, more precisely, between Poseidon and the other gods). As the Phaiakians watch their ship turned to stone, Alkinoös tells us that this is the fulfilment of a prophecy: 'Ah now, the prophecy of old is come to completion' (172). In doing so, he repeats the words of Polyphemos, just after Odysseus has revealed his name (IX.507). Odysseus' adventures and eventual return are, it seems, decreed by fate. In any case, the episode also marks the end of Poseidon's pursuit of Odysseus. Odysseus has landed in Ithaka, and the god has thus failed to thwart his *nostos*; it only remains for him to punish those who assisted him in it. Poseidon is mentioned a few more times in the poem, but only in passing.

Whether or not they are destroyed, the Phaiakians also disappear entirely from the narrative, the character of which now changes radically. There are no longer monsters and enchantresses to contend with; Odysseus is among humans again. His waking up beneath an olive tree – a symbol of life and humanity for the ancient Greeks – is highly significant, as is his ecstatic embrace of the 'grain-giving ground' when Athene finally scatters the mists and shows him Ithaka. What delights him is being among real people again, and we find them portrayed with a realism almost entirely absent from the *Iliad*. There is a practical aspect to Odysseus' transformation into a beggar, and his living among slaves and farmhands; it enables him to find out what is going on in his household, without arousing suspicion – and to take stock of his status and his relationships. As one critic has put it, 'the whole of the second half of the *Odyssey* consists in Odysseus' rediscovery of the familiar through alienation' (Segal 1962: 46). Besides this, it serves an aesthetic and structural purpose. It allows the poet to emphasise the extraordinary difference between the world Odysseus inhabited in Books V to XII and that in which he now finds himself.

Perhaps the most striking feature of Book XIII, though, is the rekindling of Odysseus' relationship with Athene. The goddess has been largely absent from Odysseus' adventures so far, and the hero grumbles about her neglect at 314–23. We know – and Athene insists (302–6) – that she was helping him during his stay with the Phaiakians, but she and Odysseus have not come face to face since he left Troy. But we know from the early books that he has always been her favorite (see, for example, Nestor's speech to Telemachos at III.218–24). Here we can see why. Both goddess and hero are clever and devious; they appear in disguise throughout the poem – the only characters to do so. Athene identifies this as the reason for their special affinity:

> since you are far the best of all mortal
> men for counsel and stories, and I among all the divinities
> am famous for wit (*mētis*) and sharpness (297–9)

This is, then, a reunion to rival that of Odysseus and Penelope – and like that reunion it is characterised by tricksiness and game-playing. Besides deceiving Odysseus as to his location, Athene also teases him in her opening speech, always telling the truth – but managing to mislead at the same time; she tells Odysseus that he '[must] have come from / far away, if you ask about this land' since 'the name of Ithaka has gone even / to Troy' (237–49). The whole encounter is characterised by trickery: the mist cast over the island, the shepherdess disguise worn by Athene, the transformation of Odysseus into a beggar at the close of the book. There is a strange intimacy – unusual in encounters between god and man – in this teasing, and the closeness between Odysseus and Athene continues after she has revealed her identity. Odysseus has no qualms about calling her plans into question, and there is perhaps even a hint of anger in his voice when the subject turns to Telemachos:

> 'Why then did you not tell him, since in your mind you know all things?
> Was it so that he too wandering over the barren
> sea should suffer pains, while others ate up his substance? (417–19)

Athene is able to pacify him, but the frustration is striking – and echoes that of some readers, who have failed to see the purpose of Telemachos' travels.

When he encounters the disguised Athene, Odysseus in turn constructs an entirely false identity. He is, he says, a Cretan, forced into exile after killing a man. This is the first of the so-called 'lying tales', which appear frequently in the second half of the poem. In each of them Odysseus claims to be from Crete (see note on 256–86 below), and in each of them he casts some light on his own mentality. Here for example, he declares himself ready to kill in defence of his own property: 'I killed him / because he tried to deprive me of all my share of my plunder / from Troy, and for the sake of it my heart suffered many / pains' (261–4). The words could be a warning to the shepherd boy, whom Odysseus perhaps suspects of having designs on his Phaiakian gifts – but equally it looks forward to the violent revenge he will exact on those who have exploited his absence; on the lying tales, see Goldhill (1991: 36–48). But the most striking thing about Odysseus' lying tales is their plausibility. Athene *knows* that Odysseus is lying, of course, but this is not (necessarily) true of his later listeners: Eumaios, Antinoös and Penelope. The realism of these fictions contrasts oddly with the fantastical 'true' events recounted in the previous four books, and – for some readers – demands that we question the accuracy of Odysseus' earlier narration.

So he spoke,* and all of them stayed stricken to silence,
held in thrall by the story all through the shadowy chambers.
Then Alkinoös answered him in turn and said to him:
'Odysseus, now that you have come to my house, bronze-founded
with the high roof, I think you will not lose your homecoming,   5
nor be driven back from it again, for all your sufferings.
Now I lay this charge upon each man of you, such as
here in my palace drink the gleaming wine of the princes
always at my side, and hear the song of the singer.
Clothing for our guest is stored away in the polished   10
chest, and intricately wrought gold, and all those other
gifts the Phaiakian men of counsel brought here to give him.
Come, let us man by man each one of us give a great tripod
and a caldron, and we will make it good to us by a collection
among the people. It is hard for a single man to be generous.'   15
   So Alkinoös spoke, and his word pleased all the rest of them.
They all went home to go to bed, each one to his own house.
But when the young Dawn showed again with her rosy fingers,
they came in haste to the ship, and brought the lavish bronze with
   them,
and Alkinoös, the hallowed prince, himself going on board,   20
stowed it well away under the thwarts, so it would not hamper
any of the crew as they rowed with their oars and sent the ship
   speedily
on. Then all went to Alkinoös' house and made the feast ready.
   Alkinoös, the hallowed prince, sacrificed an ox for them
to Zeus, dark-clouded son of Kronos, lord over all men.   25
They burned the thigh pieces and enjoyed feasting on the glorious
banquet, and among them Demodokos,* the divine singer,
sang his songs and was prized by the people. But now Odysseus
turned his head again and again to look at the shining
sun, to hasten its going down, since he was now eager   30
to go; and as a man makes for his dinner,* when all day
long his wine-colored oxen have dragged the compact plow for him
across the field, and the sun's setting is welcome for bringing
the time to go to his dinner, and as he goes his knees fail him;

---

1 **So he spoke**] Apart from a brief interruption (XI.333–77), the last four books have been
spoken by Odysseus. We learned in that interruption that Alkinoös believed Odysseus' story ('we
as we look upon you do not imagine / that you are a deceptive or thievish man' (363–4)). We also
saw Arete arguing that Odysseus be laden with gifts before his return to Ithaka; her wishes are
granted in Alkinoös' speech at the start of Book XIII.
   27 **Demodokos**] The bard of the Phaiakian court, who sang about Ares and Aphrodite, and
about the sack of Troy, in Book VIII.
   31–5 This simile has particular resonance, as the comparison is drawn from the Ithakan
landscape to which he longs to return. See p. 12 above.

thus welcome to Odysseus now was the sun going under.   35
Now he spoke aloud to the oar-loving Phaiakians,
addressing his words to Alkinoös beyond all others:
'O great Alkinoös, pre-eminent among all people,
make libation and send me upon my way untroubled;
and yourselves fare well, for all my heart desired is now made   40
good, conveyance and loving gifts. May the sky gods make these
prosper for me. May I return to my house and find there
a blameless wife, and all who are dear to me unharmed. May you
in turn, remaining here, bring comfort and cheer to your wedded
wives and your children, and may the gods grant success in every   45
endeavor, and no unhappiness be found in your people.'
   So he spoke, and they all approved his word and encouraged
convoy for the guest, for what he said was fair and orderly;
then the hallowed prince Alkinoös spoke to his herald:
'Pontonoös, now mix a bowl of wine and serve it   50
to all in the palace, so that, with a prayer to our father
Zeus, we may send our guest on his way, back to his own country.'
So he spoke, and Pontonoös mixed the sweet wine and served it
to all, standing beside each person. They poured a libation
to all the blessed immortal gods who hold wide heaven   55
from the chairs where they were sitting, but great Odysseus stood up
and put the handled goblet into the hand of Arete,
and spoke to her aloud and addressed her in winged words, saying:
'Farewell to you, O queen, and for all time, until old age
comes to you, and death, which befall all human creatures.   60
Now I am on my way; but have joy here in your household,
in your children and your people, and in your king, Alkinoös.'
   So spoke great Odysseus, and strode out over the door sill,
and great Alkinoös sent his herald to go along with him
and show him the way to the fast ship and the sand of the seashore.   65
Also Arete sent her serving women with him. One
carried a mantel, washed and clean, and a tunic. Another
one she sent along with him to carry the well-made
chest, and a third went along with them bearing food and red wine.
   But when they had come down to the sea, and where the ship
      was,   70
the proud escorts promptly took over the gifts, and stowed them
away in the hollow hull, and all the food and the drink, then
spread out a coverlet for Odysseus, and linen, out on
the deck, at the stern of the ship's hull, so that he could sleep there
undisturbed, and he himself went aboard and lay down   75
silently. They sat down each in his place at the oarlocks
in order, and slipped the cable free from its hole in the stone post.

They bent to their rowing, and with their oars tossed up the sea
  spray,
and upon the eyes of Odysseus there fell a sleep, gentle,
the sweetest kind of sleep* with no awakening, most like   80
death; while the ship, as in a field four stallions drawing
a chariot all break together at the stroke of the whiplash,
and lifting high their feet lightly beat out their path, so
the stern of this ship would lift and the creaming wave behind her
boiled amain in the thunderous crash of the sea. She ran on   85
very steady and never wavering; even the falcon,
that hawk that flies lightest of winged creatures, could not have
  paced her,
so lightly did she run on her way and cut through the sea's waves.
She carried a man with a mind like the gods for counsel, one whose
spirit up to this time had endured much, suffering many   90
pains: the wars of men, hard crossing of the big waters;
but now he slept still, oblivious of all he had suffered.

    At the time when shines that brightest star, which beyond others
comes with announcement of the light of the young Dawn goddess,
then was the time the sea-faring ship put in to the island.   95

    There is the harbor of the Old Man of the Sea, Phorkys,*
in the countryside of Ithaka. There two precipitous
promontories opposed jut out, to close in the harbor
and shelter it from the big waves made by the winds blowing
so hard on the outside; inside, the well-benched vessels   100
can lie without being tied up, once they have found their
  anchorage.
At the head of the harbor, there is an olive tree with spreading
leaves, and nearby is a cave that is shaded, and pleasant,
and sacred to the nymphs who are called the Nymphs of the
  Wellsprings,
Naiads. There are mixing bowls and handled jars inside it,   105
all of stone, and there the bees deposit their honey.
And therein also are looms that are made of stone, very long, where
the nymphs weave their sea-purple webs, a wonder to look on;
and there is water forever flowing. It has two entrances,
one of them facing the North Wind, where people can enter,   110
but the one toward the South Wind has more divinity. That is
the way of the immortals, and no men enter by that way.

78–92 Odysseus sleeps throughout his voyage back to Ithaka. This has a magical feel to it (though no divine agency is mentioned), and has been foretold by Arete at VIII.443–5. The super-natural speed of the Phaiakian ships has also been constantly hinted at (by Athene at VII.35–6, and by Arete). See XXIII.342–3.
    96 **Phorkys**] The grandfather of the Cyclops (see I.76).

It was into this bay they rowed their ship. They knew of it
   beforehand.*
The ship, hard-driven, ran up onto the beach for as much as
half her length, such was the force the hands of the oarsmen   115
gave her. They stepped from the strong-benched ship out onto the
   dry land,
and at first they lifted and carried Odysseus out of the hollow
hull, along with his bed linen and shining coverlet,
and set him down on the sand. He was still bound fast in sleep.
   Then
they lifted and carried out his possessions, those which the haughty 120
Phaiaikians, urged by the great-hearted Athene,* had given him, as
   he
set out for home, and laid them next to the trunk of olive,*
all in a pile and away from the road, lest some wayfarer
might come before Odysseus awoke, and spoil his possessions.
Then they themselves turned back toward home. But the
   Earthshaker   125
had not forgotten those threats he had once uttered at godlike
Odysseus in the beginning, and he asked Zeus for counsel:
'Father Zeus, no longer among gods immortal
shall I be honored, when there are mortals who do me no honor,
the Phaiakians, and yet these are of my own blood. See now,   130
I had said to myself Odysseus would come home only after
much suffering. I had not indeed taken away his homecoming
altogether away, since first you nodded your head and assented
to it. But they carried him asleep in the fast ship, over
the sea, and set him down in Ithaka, and gave him numberless   135
gifts, as bronze, and gold abundant, and woven clothing,
more than Odysseus could ever have taken from Troy, even
if he had come home ungrieved and with his fair share of the
   plunder.'
   Then in turn Zeus who gathers the clouds made answer:
'What a thing to have said, Earthshaker of the wide strength.   140
The gods do not hold you in dishonor. It would be a hard thing
if we were to put any slight on the eldest and best among us.

---

113 **They knew of it beforehand**] Alkinoös has told Odysseus that 'the ships themselves understand men's thoughts and purposes / and they know all the cities of men' (VIII.559–60). So the
ease of navigation is not owing to skilful steersmanship (the Phaiakian boats do not need steersmen), but to the magical properties of the ships.

121 **urged by great-hearted Athene**] She has not directly urged the Phaiakians to do anything,
but helped Odysseus to make such a favorable impression on them. She makes the claim on her
own behalf at 302–5.

116–22 The sleeping Odysseus is laid underneath an olive tree – a mark of his having returned
to the real, Greek world. His bed is also made from an olive tree; see XXIII.190–204.

But if there is any man who, giving way to the violence
and force in him, slights you, it will be yours to punish him.
Now and always. Do as you will and as it pleases you.'   145
   Then in turn Poseidon shaker of the earth made answer:
'I would act quickly, dark-clouded one, as you advise me,
but always I have respect for your anger, and keep out of
its way. This time, I wish to stun that beautiful vessel
of the Phaiakians out on the misty sea as it comes back   150
from its journey, so that they might stop, and give over conveying
people. And I would hide their city under a mountain.'*
   Then in turn Zeus who gathers the clouds made answer:
'Good brother, here is the way it seems to my mind best
to do. When all the people are watching her from the city   155
as she comes in, then turn her into a rock that looks like
a fast ship, close off shore, so that all people might wonder
at her. But do not hide their city under a mountain.'*
   When the shaker of the earth Poseidon heard him, he went off
striding to Scheria, where the Phaiakians are born and live. There   160
he waited, and the sea-going ship came close in, lightly
pursuing her way, and the Earthshaker came close up to her,
and turned her into stone and rooted her there to the bottom
with a flat stroke of his hand. And then he went away from her.
The Phaiakians of the long oars, the sea-famed people,   165
now began talking to each other and spoke in winged words;
and thus they would speak, each looking at the man next to him:
'Ah me, who was it fastened our swift ship* in the water
as she came rowing in for home? Just now she could be seen plainly.'
Thus one or another spoke but they did not know what had
   happened.   170
To them now Alkinoös spoke forth and addressed them:
'Ah now, the prophecy of old is come to completion,*
that my father spoke, when he said Poseidon someday would be
   angry

---

   152 And I would hide their city under a mountain] It appears that we are about to witness the
fulfillment of Nausithoös' prophecy, as recounted by Alkinoös at VIII.566–9. The prophecy is
repeated verbatim at 175–7.

   158 But do not hide their city under a mountain] A famously tricky passage. In the manuscripts,
Zeus tells Poseidon: 'And hide their city under a great mountain' The ancient critic Aristophanes
suggested that the word 'not' (Gk *mē*) was missing from the verse, and most modern editors
follow him. Ultimately, we never know what becomes of the Phaiakians, as the narrative cuts
away at the critical moment. We do not know whether Zeus' intercession with Poseidon has been
successful, or whether Poseidon has been won over by the Phaiakians' sacrifice. Some critics have
argued that, if the destruction of the Phaiakians' city is fated (as Alkinoös' report of the prophecy
seems to imply) then no sacrifice, or divine intervention, can prevent its happening.

   168 swift ship] The ship remains swift even when fixed in the water. See note on VI.26.

   172 Ah now . . . completion] = IX.507.

with us, because we are convoy without hurt to all men.
He said that one day, as a well-made ship of Phaiakian   175
men came back from a convoy on the misty face of the water,
he would stun it, and pile a great mountain over our city, to hide it.
So the old man spoke. Now all is being accomplished.
Come then, let us do as I say, let us all be won over.
Stop our conveying of every mortal who makes his arrival   180
here at our city. We must dedicate also to Poseidon
twelve bulls, chosen out of the herds. Then he might take pity
on us, and not pile up a high mountain over our city.'
    So he spoke, and they were afraid and made the bulls ready.
So these leaders of the Phaiakians and men of counsel   185
among their people made their prayer to the lord Poseidon,
standing around the altar. But now great Odysseus wakened
from his sleep in his own fatherland, and he did not know it,
having been long away, for the goddess, Pallas Athene,
daughter of Zeus, poured a mist over all, so she could make him   190
unrecognizable and explain all the details to him,
to have his wife not recognize him, nor his townspeople
and friends, till he punished the suitors for their overbearing
    oppression.
Therefore, to the lord Odysseus she made everything look otherwise
than it was, the penetrating roads, the harbors where all could   195
anchor, the rocks going straight up, and the trees tall growing.
He sprang and stood upright and looked about at his native
country, and groaned aloud and struck himself on both thighs
with the flats of his hands, and spoke a word of lamentation:
'Ah me,* what are these people whose land I have come to this
    time,   200
and are they savage and violent, and without justice,
or hospitable to strangers and with minds that are godly?
And where shall I take all these many goods? Where shall I
myself be driven? I wish I had stayed among the Phaiakians,
just where I was, and I would have visited some other powerful   205
king, who then would have been my friend and seen to my journey.
Now I do not know where to put all this, and I cannot
leave it here, for fear it may become spoil for others.
Shame on the leaders of the Phaiakians and their men of counsel,
for they were not altogether thoughtful, nor were they righteous,   210
when they took me away here to another land; but they told me
they would being me to sunny Ithaka, and they did not do it.

200–2 **Ah me . . . justice**] As on the Scherian coast, Odysseus has just woken up in a strange land, and has no clear sense of what reception to expect. See: VI.119–21; and IX.175–6.

May Zeus of the suppliants punish them,* for he oversees other
men besides, and punishes anyone who transgresses.
But come, let me count my goods and find out whether they might
   not   215
have gone taking some of it with them in the hollow vessel.'
   So speaking, he counted up the surpassingly beautiful tripods
and caldrons, and the gold and all the fine woven clothing.
There was nothing gone from all this; but he in great sorrow
crept over the beach of his own country beside the resounding   220
sea, with much lamentation; but now Athene came near him
likening herself in form to a young man, a herdsman
of sheep, a delicate boy, such as the children of kings are,
and wearing a well-wrought shawl in a double fold over her
   shoulders.
Under her shining feet she had sandals, and in her hand carried   225
a spear. Odysseus, in joy at the sight, came up to meet her,
and spoke aloud to her and addressed her in winged words, saying:
'Dear friend, since you are the first I have met with in this country,
I give you greeting. Do not cross me with evil purpose,
but rescue these possessions and me. I make prayer to you   230
as to a god, and come to your dear knees as a suppliant.
And tell me this and tell me truly, so that I may know it.
What land is this, what neighborhood is it, what people live here?
Is it some one of the sunny islands, or is it some foreland
slanted out from the generous mainland into the salt sea?'   235
   Then in turn the gray-eyed Athene answered:
'You are some innocent, O stranger, or else you have come from
far away, if you ask about this land, for it is not
so nameless as all that. There are indeed many who know it,
whether among those who live toward east and the sunrise,   240
or those who live up and away toward the mist and darkness. See
   now,
this is a rugged country and not for the driving of horses,
but neither is it so unpleasant, though not widely shapen;
for there is abundant grain for bread grown here, it produces
wine, and there is always rain and the dew to make it   245
fertile; it is good to feed goats and cattle; and timber
is there of all sorts, and watering places good through the seasons;
so that, stranger, the name of Ithaka has gone even
to Troy, though they say that is very far from Achaian country.'
   So she spoke, and resourceful great Odysseus was happy,   250

---

213 **May Zeus of the suppliants punish them**] The Phaiakians have already been punished –
ironically for their over-attentiveness to *xeinoi*.

rejoicing in the land of his fathers when Pallas Athene
daughter of Zeus of the aegis told him the truth of it,
and so he answered her again and addressed her in winged words;
but he did not tell her the truth, but checked that word from the
    outset,
forever using to every advantage the mind that was in him:*   255
'I heard the name of Ithaka when I was in wide Crete,*
far away across the sea, now I myself have come here
with those goods that you see, but leaving as much again to my
    children.
I have fled, an exile, because I killed the son of Idomeneus,*
Orsilochos, a man swift of foot, who in wide Crete surpassed   260
all other mortal men for speed of his feet. I killed him
because he tried to deprive me of all my share of the plunder
from Troy, and for the sake of it my heart suffered many
pains: the wars of men; hard crossing of the big waters;
for I would not do his father favor, and serve as his henchman   265
in the land of Troy, but I led others, of my own following.
I lay in wait for him with a friend by the road, and struck him
with the bronze-headed spear as he came back from the fields. There
    was
a very dark night spread over all the sky, nor did anyone
see me, nor did anyone know of it when I stripped the life   270
from him. But then, when I had cut him down with the sharp bronze,
I went at once to a ship, and supplicated the lordly
Phoenician men, and gave them spoil, to stay their eagerness,
and asked them to carry me and to set me down in Pylos
or shining Elis where the Epeians are lords: but it happened   275
that the force of the wind beat them away from those places, greatly
against their will; it was not as if they wished to deceive me.
So, driven off those courses, we came in here, by night,
and rowed hastily into the harbor, nor was there any
thought in us of the evening meal, much though we wanted it,   280
but all of us came off the ship as we were, and lay down;
then, weary as I was, the sweetness of sleep came upon me,
while they, taking all the possessions out of the hollow hull, set them
ashore on the sand, and close to the place where I was lying,

---

255 **using to every advantage the mind that was in him**] Another instance of the strange nature of Odysseus' heroism.

256–86 This is the first of five 'lying tales' told by Odysseus in the second half of the poem. The others are at XIV.192–359 (to Eumaios), XVII.415–44 (to Antinoös), XIX.165–299 (to Penelope), and XXIV.244–314 (to Laertes). On each of these occasions he claims to have come from Crete; there is a possible significance to this, in that Cretans were regarded as proverbially dishonest.

259 **Idomeneus**] Odysseus later claims to be Idomeneus' brother (XIX.181).

and they, embarking, went on their way to strongly settled   285
Sidon; but I, grieving at the heart, was left behind here.'
    So he spoke. The goddess, gray-eyed Athene, smiled on him,
and stroked him with her hand, and took on the shape of a woman
both beautiful and tall, and well versed in glorious handiworks,
and spoke aloud to him and addressed him in winged words, saying: 290
'It would be a sharp one, and a stealthy one, who would ever get
    past you
in any contriving; even if it were a god against you.
You wretch, so devious, never weary of tricks, then you would not
even in your own country give over your ways of deceiving
and your thievish tales. They are near to you in your very nature.   295
But come, let us talk no more of this, for you and I both know
sharp practice, since you are far the best of all mortal
men for counsel and stories, and I among all the divinities
am famous for wit and sharpness; and yet you never recognized
Pallas Athene, daughter of Zeus, the one who is always   300
standing beside you and guarding you in every endeavor.
And it was I who made you loved by all the Phaiakians.
And now again I am here, to help you in your devising
of schemes, and hide the possessions which the haughty Phaiakians
bestowed – it was by my thought and counsel – on you, as you
    started   305
for home, and tell you all the troubles you are destined to suffer
in your well-wrought house; but you must, of necessity, endure
all, and tell no one out of all the men and women
that you have come back from your wandering, but you must
    endure
much grief in silence, standing and facing men in their violence.' 310
    Then in turn resourceful Odysseus spoke to her in answer:
'It is hard, O goddess, for even a man of good understanding
to recognize you on meeting, for you take every shape upon you.
But this I know well: there was a time when you were kind to me
in the days when we sons of the Achaians were fighting in Troy land. 315
But after we had sacked the sheer citadel of Priam,
and went away in our ships, and the god scattered the Achaians
I never saw you, Daughter of Zeus, after that, nor did I
know of your visiting my ship, to beat off some trouble
from me, but always with my heart torn inside its coverings   320
I wandered, until the gods set me free from unhappiness, until
in the rich territory of the Phaiakian men you cheered me
with words, then led me, yourself in person, into their city.
And now I entreat you in the name of your father; for I do not think
I have really come into sunny Ithaka, but have been driven   325

off course to another country, and I think you are teasing me
when you tell me I am, and saying it to beguile me; tell me
if it is true that I have come back to my own dear country.'
    Then in turn the goddess gray-eyed Athene answered him,
'Always you are the same, and such is the mind within you,   330
and so I cannot abandon you when you are unhappy,
because you are fluent, and reason closely, and keep your head
    always.
Anyone else come home from wandering would have run happily
off to see his children and wife in his halls; but it is not
your pleasure to investigate and ask questions, not till   335
you have made trial of your wife; yet she, as always,
sits there in your palace, and always with her the wretched
nights, and the days also, waste her away with weeping.
And I never did have any doubt, but in my heart always
knew how you would come home, having lost all of your
    companions.   340
But, you see, I did not want to fight with my father's
brother, Poseidon, who was holding a grudge against you
in his heart, and because you blinded his dear son,* hated you.
Come, I will show you settled Ithaka, so you will believe me.
This is the harbor of the Old Man of the sea, Phorkys,   345
and here at the head of the harbor is the olive tree with spreading
leaves, and nearby is the cave that is shaded, and pleasant,
and sacred to the nymphs, who are called the Nymphs of the
    Wellsprings,
Naiads. That is the wide over-arching cave, where often
you used to accomplish for the nymphs their complete hecatombs;   350
and there is the mountain, Neritos, all covered with forest.'
    So speaking the goddess scattered the mist, and the land was
    visible.
Long-suffering great Odysseus was gladdened then, rejoicing
in the sight of his country, and kissed the grain-giving ground,
    then
raised his hands in the air and spoke to the nymphs, praying: 355
'Naiad nymphs, O daughters of Zeus, I never suspected
that I would see you again. Be welcome now to my gentle
prayers, but I will also give you gifts, as I used to
before, if Athene the Spoiler, Zeus' daughter, freely grants me
to go on living here myself, and sustains my dear son.'   360
    Then in turn the goddess gray-eyed Athene said to him:
'Never fear, let none of these matters trouble your mind. Rather

343 **his dear son**] Polyphemos.

let us hide these possessions without delay, deep in the inward
part of the wonderful cave, so they will be kept safe for you.
Then we shall make our plans how all may come out best for us.'   365
   So the goddess spoke, and went inside the shadowy
cave, looking through it for hiding places. Meanwhile, Odysseus
brought everything close up, gold, tireless bronze, clothing
that had been made with care, given him by the Phaiakians,
and stowed it well away inside; and Pallas Athene,   370
daughter of Zeus of the aegis, set a stone against the doorway.
   The two sat down against the trunk of the hallowed olive,
and plotted out the destruction of the overmastering suitors.
Their discourse was begun by the goddess gray-eyed Athene:
'Son of Laertes and seed of Zeus, resourceful Odysseus,   375
consider how you can lay your hands on these shameless suitors,
who for three years now have been as lords in your palace,
and courting your godlike wife, and offering gifts to win her.
And she, though her heart forever grieves over your homecoming,
holds out some hope for all, and makes promises to each man,   380
sending them messages, but her mind has other intentions.'
   Then resourceful Odysseus spoke in turn and answered her.
'Surely I was on the point of perishing by an evil
fate in my palace, like Atreus' son Agamemnon, unless
you had told me, goddess, the very truth of all that has happened.   385
Come then, weave the design, the way I shall take my vengeance
upon them; stand beside me, inspire me with strength and
   courage,
as when together we brought down Troy's shining coronal.
For if in your fury, O gray-eyed goddess, you stood beside me,
I would fight, lady and goddess, with your help against three
   hundred   390
men if you, freely and in full heart, would help me.'
   Then in turn the goddess gray-eyed Athene answered:
'I will indeed be at your side, you will not be forgotten
at the time when we two go to this work, and I look for endless
ground to be spattered by the blood and brains of the suitors,   395
these men who are eating all your substance away. But come
   now,
let me make you so that no mortal can recognize you.
For I will wither the handsome flesh that is on your flexible
limbs, and ruin the brown hair on your head, and about you
put on such a clout of cloth any man will loathe you when he sees
   you   400
wearing it; I will dim those eyes, that have been so handsome,
so you will be unprepossessing to all the suitors

and your wife and child, those whom you left behind in your
   palace.
First of all, you are to make your way to the swineherd
who is in charge of your pigs, but always his thoughts are kindly,   405
and he is friend to your son and to circumspect Penelope.
You will find him posted beside his pigs, and these are herded
near the Rock of the Raven and beside the spring Arethousa,
to eat the acorns that stay their strength, and drink of the darkling
water, for these are nourishing for pigs, and fatten them.   410
There you shall wait, and stay with him, and ask him all questions,
while I go over to Sparta, the country of lovely women,
and call back Telemachos, your own dear son, Odysseus,
who went into spacious Lakedaimon to see Menelaos
and ask him for news of you, and whether you were still living.'   415
   Then resourceful Odysseus spoke in turn and answered her:
'Why then did you not tell him, since in your mind you know all
   things?
Was it so that he too wandering over the barren
sea should suffer pains, while others ate up his substance?'
   Then in turn the goddess gray-eyed Athene answered: 420
'Let him not be too much on your mind. It was I myself
who saw him along on that journey, so he would win reputation
by going there, and he has no hardship, but now is staying
at his ease with the son of Atreus, and all abundance is by him.
It is true that the young men with their black ships are lying   425
in wait for him to kill him before he reaches his country;
but I think this will not happen, but that sooner the earth will
   cover
some one of those suitors, who now are eating away your
   substance.'
   So spoke Athene, and with her wand she tapped Odysseus,
and withered the handsome flesh that was upon his flexible   430
limbs, and ruined the brown hair on his head, and about him
to cover all his body she put on the skin of an ancient
old man, and then she dimmed those eyes that had been so
   handsome.
Then she put another vile rag on him, and a tunic,
tattered, squalid, blackened with the foul smoke, and over it   435
gave him the big hide of a fast-running deer, with the hairs
   rubbed
off, to wear, and she gave him a staff, and an ugly wallet
that was full of holes, with a twist of rope attached, to dangle it.
   So they two consulted and went their ways. The goddess
went to bright Lakedaimon to fetch the son of Odysseus.   440

Book XXIII: Odysseus and Penelope

Much of the poem so far has focused on the concealment and revela-
tion of the hero's identity. Here, for the first time, he is recognised as
Odysseus, in his own household. But, at the same time, there is something potentially disturbing about the manner of his return. Penelope
has not seen her husband for twenty years. She is woken up by a
maid, and told that he has returned, and that he has killed the men
who had been afflicting her. Her reaction – understandably – is one
of uncertainty, and this uncertainty is beautifully captured. She is led
through the house – still not fully awakened from the deepest sleep
she has experienced in twenty years – and brought face to face with a
man who claims to be her husband. He is dripping with blood. As one
might expect, many recent writers have chosen to focus on Penelope's
situation, rather than Odysseus'. Margaret Atwood, in her *Penelopiad*
(2005), presents a Penelope whose circumspection shades into cyni-
cism, and who plays along with her returning husband, despite being
appalled by the violence he brings to the household: 'I decided to make
him wait: I myself had waited long enough. Also I need time in order
to fully disguise my true feelings about the unfortunate hanging of my
twelve young maids' (169). This reading is a compelling one, but only
one of many. Penelope's behaviour in Book XXIII is susceptible to an
enormous range of interpretations – which is one reason why it has
provided such fertile ground for poets and novelists (on which see Hall
2008: esp. 115–29).

Readers of the *Odyssey* have been divided, in particular, on the exact
moment at which Penelope recognises her husband. She learns at a
fairly early stage that 'a stranger, some unfortunate man' is in the house
(XVII.502). She talks at length with Odysseus – disguised as the beggar
– about his knowledge of her husband; he assures her that Odysseus
is 'close at hand' (XIX.301). When instructing Eurykleia to bathe the
beggar, she tells him that 'Odysseus / must by this time have just such
hands and feet as you do, / for in misfortune mortal men grow old more
suddenly' (XIX.358–60). In Book XXIII, she refuses to accept that
Odysseus has returned – even when she has heard about the scar on his
thigh. Only when he shows knowledge of the interior of their bedroom
does she acknowledge him. Irony and suspense pervade these encounters
– but to what extent can we regard Penelope as the author of this irony
and suspense (as we can Odysseus)? Is it possible that she was aware of
the beggar's identity all along, and instituted the axe-test knowing what
would happen (the dead suitors certainly think so in Book XXIV)? A

large strand of criticism (often, though not always, by feminist critics) has sought to grant autonomy to Penelope – traditionally regarded chiefly as a passive exemplar of female chastity. See, for example: Amory 1963; Austin 1975; Katz 1991; Felson-Rubin 1994. Hall 2008: 126–30 gives a useful summary of the literature.

At the heart of the book is the trick by which Penelope establishes, beyond all doubt, that this blood-spattered man is Odysseus; the request that the bed be moved from their room. According to one reading – which views the episode in a subtly different light from the critics mentioned above – Penelope's trick reinforces the fact that up until this point the story has been 'told one-sidedly from the point of view of male anxiety and only when Penelope tricks Odysseus do we realise how one-sided the telling has been' (Winkler 1990: 159). It also reminds the audience that *mētis* is as much a part of Penelope's character as it is of Odysseus'. For three years, she managed to keep the suitors skillfully at bay by telling them she would remarry only when she has finished weaving a winding-sheet for Odysseus' father – but what she weaves by day, she unpicks by night (described at II.93–109; XIX.137–55; XXIV.128–45). Penelope's outsmarting of Odysseus (whether it is momentary, or the culmination of a campaign of trickery) indicates their suitability for one another. And in the simile that follows, at the moment of their final reunion, their identities seem to fuse; Penelope's joy and relief are described in terms which recall Odysseus' reaching the Phaiakian coast (333–40).

There are various other roles that Penelope might have played – most notably those of Klytaimestra and Helen. Agamemnon, when he appears in the underworld in Book XXIV, praises Penelope, and draws a contrast with his own wife:

> the immortals will make for the people
> of earth a thing of grace in the song for prudent Penelope.
> Not so did the daughter of Tyndareos [Klytaimestra] fashion her evil
> deeds, when she killed her wedded lord, and a song of loathing
> will be hers among men, to make evil the reputation
> of womankind, even for ones whose acts are virtuous. (XXIV.197–202)

This is the final consummation of the parallel initiated in Book I. Agamemnon's family were there held up as a negative example – an instance of what might befall the House of Ithaka if they its members were unfortunate or inert; Agamemnon himself now confirms that such a fate has been avoided.

The old woman,* laughing loudly, went to the upper chamber
to tell her mistress that her beloved husband was inside
the house. Her knees moved swiftly, but her feet were tottering.
She stood above Penelope's head and spoke a word with her:
'Wake, Penelope,* dear child, so that, with your own eyes,   5
you can see what all your days you have been longing for.
Odysseus is here, he is in the house, though late in his coming;
and he has killed the haughty suitors, who were afflicting
his house, and using force on his son, and eating his property.'
    Circumspect Penelope* said to her in answer: 10
'Dear nurse, the gods have driven you crazy. They are both able
to change a very sensible person into a senseless
one, and to set the light-wit on the way of discretion.
They have set you awry; before now your thoughts were orderly.
Why do you insult me when my heart is heavy with sorrows,   15
by talking in this wild way, and waking me from a happy
sleep,* which had come and covered my eyes, and held them
    fastened?
For I have not had such a sleep as this one, since the time
when Odysseus went to that evil, not-to-be-mentioned Ilion.
But go down now, and take yourself back into the palace.   20
If any of those other women, who are here with me,
had come with a message like yours, and wakened me from my
    slumber,
I would have sent her back on her way to the hall in a hateful
fashion for doing it. It shall be your age that saves you.'
    Then the beloved nurse Eurykleia said to her in answer: 25
'I am not insulting you, dear child. It is all true.
Odysseus is here, he is in the house, just as I tell you.
He is that stranger-guest, whom all in the house were abusing.
Telemachos has known that he was here for a long time,
but he was discreet, and did not betray the plans of his father,   30
so he might punish these overbearing men for their violence.'
    So she spoke, and Penelope in her joy sprang up

1 **The old woman**] Eurykleia, Odysseus' nurse. She is laughing loudly because she is so
delighted by her master's slaughter of the suitors, recounted in gruesome detail in the previous
book. At the close of that book, Odysseus ordered her to fetch Penelope.

5 **Wake, Penelope**] Telemachos sent Penelope to bed at the end of Book XXI, so she is unaware
that the suitors have been killed.

10 **Circumspect Penelope**] Circumspect (Gk *periphrōn*) is the epithet most frequently applied to
Penelope. If she has been circumspect towards the suitors, then she is even more so in her dealings
with Odysseus – and, most immediately, with Eurykleia, who struggles to persuade her that her
husband has returned.

16–17 **waking me from a happy / sleep**] Penelope has told the disguised Odysseus (at XIX.515–
24) that her nights are troubled. Now, for the first time in twenty years, she is sleeping deeply – as
though responding intuitively to developments in the household.

from the bed, and embraced the old woman, her eyes streaming
tears, and she spoke to her and addressed her in winged words:
'Come, dear nurse, and give me a true account of the matter,   35
whether he really has come back to his house, as you tell me,
to lay his hands on the shameless suitors, though he was only
one, and they were always lying in wait, in a body!'
  Then the beloved nurse Eurykleia said to her in answer:
'I did not see, I was not told, but I heard an outcry   40
of them being killed; we, hidden away in the strong-built
    storerooms,
sat there terrified, and the closed doors held us prisoner,
until from inside the great hall your son Telemachos
summoned me, because his father told him to do it.
There I found Odysseus standing among the dead men   45
he had killed, and they covered the hardened earth, lying
piled on each other around him. You would have been cheered* to
    see him,
spattered over with gore and battle filth, like a lion.
Now they lie all together, by the doors of the courtyard,
while he is burning a great fire, and cleaning the beautiful   50
house with brimstone.* He has sent me on to summon you.
Come with me then, so that both of you can turn your dear hearts
the way of happiness, since you have had so much to suffer,
but now at last what long you prayed for has been accomplished.
He has come back and is here at his hearth, alive, and has found you   55
and his son in the palace, and has taken revenge on the suitors
here in his house, for all the evils that they have done him.'
  Circumspect Penelope said to her in answer:
'Dear nurse, do not yet laugh aloud in triumph.* You know
how welcome he would be if he appeared in the palace: 60
to all, but above all to me and the son we gave birth to.
No, but this story is not true as you tell it; rather,
some one of the immortals has killed the haughty suitors
in anger over their wicked deeds and heart-hurting violence;
for these men paid no attention at all to any man on earth   65
who came their way, no matter if he were base or noble.
So they suffered for their own recklessness. But Odysseus
has lost his homecoming and lost his life, far from Achaia.'

---

47 **You would have been cheered**] Odysseus has admonished Eurykleia at XXII.411–17, for taking too much pleasure in the death of the suitors.

50–1 **cleaning the beautiful house / with brimstone**] Another of the domestic details so frequent in the poem. Odysseus himself is cleaning up after the battle.

59 **do not yet laugh aloud in triumph**] Penelope seems to echo Odysseus' words, although her point is rather different. She assumes that Odysseus is dead, and that the suitors must have been killed by divine agency – and it is therefore wrong to take pride in the events.

Then the beloved nurse Eurykleia said to her in answer:
'My child, what sort of word escaped your teeth's barrier?   70
Though your husband is here beside the hearth, you would never
say he would come home. Your heart was always mistrustful.*
But here is another proof that is very clear. I will tell you.
That scar,* which once the boar with his white teeth inflicted.
I recognized it while I was washing his feet, and I wanted   75
to tell you about it, but he stopped my mouth with his hands, would not
let me speak, for his mind sought every advantage.* Come then,
follow me, and I will hazard my life upon it.
Kill me by the most pitiful death, if I am deceiving you.'
    Circumspect Penelope said to her in answer: 80
'Dear nurse,* it would be hard for you to baffle the purposes
of the everlasting gods, although you are very clever.
Still, I will go to see my son, so that I can look on
these men who courted me lying dead, and the man who killed
them'.
    She spoke, and came down from the chamber, her heart pondering 85
much, whether* to keep away and question her dear husband,
or to go up to him and kiss his head, taking his hands.
But then, when she came in and stepped over the stone threshold,
she sat across from him in the firelight, facing Odysseus,
by the opposite wall, while he was seated by the tall pillar,   90
looking downward, and waiting to find out if his majestic
wife would have anything to say to him, now that she saw him.
She sat a long time in silence, and her heart was wondering.
Sometimes she would look at him, with her eyes full upon him,
and again would fail to know him in the foul clothing he wore.   95
Telemachos spoke to her and called her by name and scolded her:
'My mother, my harsh mother with the hard heart inside you,
why do you withdraw so from my father, and do not,
sit beside him and ask him questions and find out about him?
No other woman, with spirit as stubborn as yours, would keep back 100

72 **Your heart was always mistrustful**] Penelope's circumspection is something she has in common with her husband. See (for example) XIII.330, where Athene chastises Odysseus for needing to make trial of Penelope: 'Always you are the same, and such is the mind within you . . .'

74 **That scar**] Eurykleia recognised the scar while bathing Odysseus at XIX.467–72.

77 **for his mind sought every advantage**] This is an odd turn of phrase, echoing the description of Odysseus at XIII.255, 'forever using to every advantage the mind that was in him'.

81–2 **Dear nurse . . . very clever**] The sense of Penelope's remark is unclear. She is perhaps referring back to her lines 63–4, and her theory that one of the gods has killed the suitors. The unusual Gk word *eirusthai*, which Lattimore translates 'baffle', probably means something like 'penetrate' or 'understand'.

85–6 **pondering / much, whether**] Penelope here contemplates two alternatives, but then does something else entirely – evidence of her anxious state of mind?

as you are doing from her husband who, after much suffering,
came at last in the twentieth year back to his own country.
But always you have a heart that is harder than stone within you.'
    Circumspect Penelope said to him in answer:
'My child, the spirit that is in me is full of wonderment,   105
and I cannot find anything to say to him, nor question him,
nor look him straight in the face. But if he is truly Odysseus,
and he has come home, then we shall find other ways, and better,
to recognize each other, for we have signs that we know of
between the two of us only, but they are secrets from others.'   110
    So she spoke, and much-enduring noble Odysseus
smiled, and presently spoke in winged words to Telemachos:
'Telemachos, leave your mother to examine me in the palace
as she will, and presently she will understand better;
but now that I am dirty and wear foul clothing upon me,   115
she dislikes me for that, and says I am not her husband.
But let us make our plans how all will come out best for us.
For when one has killed only one man in a community,
and then there are not many avengers to follow, even
so, he flees into exile, leaving kinsmen and country.   120
But we killed what held the city together, the finest
young men in Ithaka. It is what I would have you consider.'
    Then the thoughtful Telemachos said to him in answer:
'You must look to this yourself, dear father; for they say
you have the best mind among men for craft, and there is   125
no other man among mortal men who can contend with you.
we shall follow you eagerly;* I think that we shall not
come short in warcraft, in so far as the strength stays with us.'
    Then resourceful Odysseus spoke in turn and answered him:
'So I will tell you the way of it, how it seems best to me.   130
First, all go and wash, and put your tunics upon you,
and tell the women in the palace to loose out their clothing.
Then let the inspired singer take his clear-sounding lyre,
and give us the lead for festive dance, so that anyone
who is outside, some one of the neighbors, or a person going   135
along the street, who hears us, will think we are having a wedding.
Let no rumor go abroad in the town that the suitors
have been murdered, until such time as we can make our way
out to our estate with its many trees, and once there
see what profitable plan the Olympian shows us.'   140
    So he spoke, and they listened well to him and obeyed him.

127–8 These lines also appear at *Iliad* XIII.785–6. Some scholars think they are a late addition to this passage.

First they went and washed, and put their tunics upon them,
and the women arrayed themselves in their finery, while the inspired
singer took up his hollowed lyre and stirred up within them
the impulse for the sweetness of song and the stately dancing.   145
Now the great house resounded aloud to the thud of their footsteps,
as the men celebrated there, and the fair-girdled women;
and thus would a person speak outside the house who heard them:
'Surely now someone has married our much-sought-after
queen; hard-hearted, she had no patience to keep the great house   150
for her own wedded lord to the end, till he came back to her.'
    So would a person speak, but they did not know what had happened.
Now the housekeeper Eurynome bathed great-hearted
Odysseus in his own house, and anointed him with olive oil,
and threw a beautiful mantle and a tunic about him;   155
and over his head Athene suffused great beauty,* to make him
taller to behold and thicker, and on his head she arranged
the curling locks that hung down like hyacinthine petals.
And as when a master craftsman overlays gold on silver,
and he is one who was taught by Hephaistos and Pallas Athene   160
in art complete, and grace is on every work he finishes;
so Athene gilded with grace his head and his shoulders.
Then looking like an immortal, he strode forth from the bath,
and came back then and sat on the chair from which he had risen,
opposite his wife, and now he spoke to her, saying: 165
'You are so strange. The gods, who have their homes on Olympos,
have made your heart more stubborn than for the rest of
    womankind.
No other woman,* with spirit as stubborn as yours, would keep
    back
as you are doing from her husband who, after much suffering,
came at last in the twentieth year back to his own country.   170
Come then, nurse, make me up a bed, so that I can use it
here; for this woman has a heart of iron within her'.
    Circumspect Penelope said to him in answer:
'You are so strange. I am not being proud, nor indifferent,
nor puzzled beyond need, but I know very well what you looked like 175
when you went in the ship with the sweeping oars, from Ithaka.
Come then, Eurykleia, and make up a firm bed for him
outside the well-fashioned chamber: that very bed that he himself

156–61 These lines are identical to those at VI.229–35, when Odysseus is on the Scherian coast.
The repetition is a fleeting reminder of his dalliance with Nausikaa. This time, he is made handsome for his wife's benefit.

168 **No other woman . . . after much suffering**] Odysseus repeats the words his son has spoken
at 102–3.

built. Put the firm bed here outside for him, and cover it
over with fleeces and blankets, and with shining coverlets.'   180
   So she spoke to her husband, trying him out, but Odysseus
spoke in anger to his virtuous-minded lady:
'What you have said, dear lady, has hurt my heart deeply. What
   man
has put my bed in another place? But it would be difficult
for even a very expert one, unless a god, coming   185
to help in person, were easily to change its position.
But there is no mortal man alive, no strong man, who lightly
could move the weight elsewhere. There is one particular feature
in the bed's construction. I myself, no other man, made it.
There was the bole of an olive tree* with long leaves growing   190
strongly in the courtyard, and it was thick, like a column.
I laid down my chamber around this, and built it, until I
finished it, with close-set stones, and roofed it well over,
and added the compacted doors, fitting closely together.
Then I cut away the foliage of the long-leaved olive,   195
and trimmed the trunk from the roots up, planning it with a brazen
adze, well and expertly, and trued it straight to a chalkline,
making a bed post of it, and bored all holes with an auger.
I began with this and built my bed, until it was finished,
and decorated it with gold and silver and ivory.   200
Then I lashed it with thongs of oxhide, dyed bright with purple.
There is its character, as I tell you; but I do not know now,
dear lady, whether my bed is still in place, or if some man
has cut underneath the stump of the olive, and moved it elsewhere.'
   So he spoke, and her knees and the heart within her went slack   205
as she recognized the clear proofs that Odysseus had given;
but then she burst into tears and ran straight to him, throwing
her arms around the neck of Odysseus, and kissed his head,* saying:
'Do not be angry with me, Odysseus, since, beyond other men,
you have the most understanding. The gods granted us misery,   210
in jealousy over the thought that we two, always together,
should enjoy our youth, and then come to the threshold of old age.
Then do not be angry with me nor blame me, because
I did not greet you, as I do now, at first when I saw you.
For always the spirit deep in my very heart was fearful   215
that some one of mortal men would come my way and deceive me
with words. For there are many who scheme for wicked advantage.

190–201 The account of how Odysseus made his bed is wonderfully precise; there is hardly
another epic hero one can imagine giving this speech – or indeed being as skilful with an adze as
he is on the battlefield.
   208 **kissed his head**] Penelope considered doing this at 87.

For neither would the daughter born to Zeus, Helen of Argos,*
have lain in love with an outlander from another country,
if she had known that the warlike sons of the Achaians would bring
   her   220
home again to the beloved land of her fathers.
It was a god who stirred her to do the shameful thing she
did, and never before had she had in her heart this terrible
wildness, out of which came suffering to us also.
But now, since you have given me accurate proof describing   225
our bed, which no other mortal man beside has ever seen,
but only you and I, and there is one serving woman,
Aktor's daughter, whom my father gave me when I came here,
who used to guard the doors for us in our well-built chamber;
so you persuade my heart, though it has been very stubborn.'   230
    She spoke, and still more roused in him the passion for weeping.
He wept as he held his lovely wife, whose thoughts were virtuous.
And as when the land* appears welcome to men who are swimming,
after Poseidon has smashed their strong-built ship on the open
water, pounding it with the weight of wind and the heavy   235
seas, and only a few escape the gray water landward
by swimming, with a thick scurf of salt coated upon them,
and gladly they set foot on the shore, escaping the evil;
so welcome was her husband to her as she looked upon him,
and she could not let him go from the embrace of her white arms.   240
Now Dawn of the rosy fingers would have dawned on their
   weeping,
had not the gray-eyed goddess Athene planned it otherwise.
She held the long night back at the outward edge, she detained
Dawn of the golden throne by the Ocean, and would not let her
harness her fast-footed horses who bring the daylight to people: 245
Lampos and Phaethon, the Dawn's horses, who carry her.
Then resourceful Odysseus spoke to his wife, saying:
'Dear wife, we have not yet come to the limit of all our
trials. There is unmeasured labor left for the future,
both difficult and great, and all of it I must accomplish.   250
So the soul of Teiresias prophesied to me, on that day
when I went down inside the house of Hades, seeking

218–24 **Penelope's defence of Helen** is strange, and some scholars have argued that it is spurious. It has the effect (although Penelope never makes this explicit) of offering an emblem of marital infidelity, against which her own steadfastness can be judged.

233–40 **And as when the land . . . her white arms**] An extraordinary simile; the audience gets a jolt on realising that Penelope, and not Odysseus, is its subject. Her feelings of relief and elation on recognising Odysseus are compared to those experienced by a shipwrecked sailor as he struggles to the shore. The comparison is clearly drawn not from Penelope's range of experience but from Odysseus', and evokes in particular the moment when he reaches the Scherian coast.

to learn about homecoming, for myself and for my companions.
but come, my wife, let us go to bed, so that at long last
we can enjoy the sweetness of slumber, sleeping together.'   255
   Circumspect Penelope said to him in answer:
'You shall have your going to bed whenever the spirit
desires it, now that the gods have brought about your homecoming
to your own strong-founded house and to the land of your fathers.
but since the gods put this into your mind, and you understand it,   260
tell me what this trial is, since I think I shall hear of it
later; so it will be none the worse if I now hear of it.'
   Then in turn resourceful Odysseus said to her in answer:
'You are so strange. Why do you urge me on and tell me
to speak of it? Yet I will tell you, concealing nothing.   265
Your heart will have no joy in this; and I myself am not
happy, since he told me to go among many cities
of men, taking my well-shaped oar in my hands and bearing it,*
until I come where there are men living who know nothing
of the sea, and who eat food that is not mixed with salt, who never   270
have known ships whose cheeks are painted purple, who never
have known well-shaped oars, which act for ships as wings do.
And then he told me a very clear proof. I will not conceal it.
When, as I walk, some other wayfarer happens to meet me,
and says I carry a winnow fan on my bright shoulder,   275
then I must plant my well-shaped oar in the ground, and render
ceremonious sacrifice to the lord Poseidon,
one ram and one bull, and a mounter of sows, a boar pig,
and make my way home again, and render holy hecatombs
to the immortal gods who hold the wide heaven, all   280
of them in order. Death will come to me from the sea, in
some altogether unwarlike way, and it will end me
in the ebbing time of a sleek old age. My people
about me will prosper. All this he told me would be accomplished.'
   Circumspect Penelope said to him in answer: 285
'If the gods are accomplishing a more prosperous old age,
then there is hope that you shall have an escape from your troubles.'
   Now as these two were conversing thus with each other,
meanwhile the nurse and Eurynome were making the bed up
with soft coverings, under the light of their flaring torches.   290
Then when they had worked and presently had a firm bed made,
the old woman went away back to bed in her own place,
while Eurynome, as mistress of the chamber, guided them
on their way to the bed, and her hands held the torch for them.

268–84 These lines are repeated (with slight alterations) from Teiresias' speech at XI.122–36.

When she had brought them to the chamber she went back. They
   then   295
gladly went together to bed, and their old ritual.*
At this time Telemachos and the oxherd and swineherd
stopped the beat of their feet in the dance, and stopped the women,
and they themselves went to bed in the shadowy palace.
   When Penelope and Odysseus had enjoyed their lovemaking,   300
they took pleasure in talking, each one telling his story.
She, shining among women, told of all she had endured
in the palace, as she watched the suitors, a ravening company,
who on her account were slaughtering many oxen
and fat sheep, and much wine was being drawn from the wine jars. 305
But shining Odysseus told of all the cares he inflicted
on other men, and told too of all that in his misery
he had toiled through. She listened to him with delight, nor did any
sleep fall upon her eyes until he had told her everything.
   He began with how he had beaten the Kikonians,* and then   310
gone to the rich country of the men who feed on the lotus.
He told all that the Cylops had done, and how he took vengeance
on him for his strong companions he had eaten, and showed no pity.
How he came to Aiolos, who generously received him
and gave him passage, but it was not fated for him to come back   315
yet to his country, so the stormwinds caught and carried him
out again on the sea where the fish swarm, groaning heavily;
and how he came to Telepylos of the Laistrygones,
and these men had destroyed his ships and strong-greaved
   companions
[all; but Odysseus only got away with his black ship].*   320
He told her of the guile and the many devices of Circe,
and how he had gone into the moldering home of Hades,
there to consult the soul of Theban Teiresias, going
in his ship with many benches, and there saw all his companions,
and his mother, who had borne him and nursed him when he was
   little.   325

---

296 **their old ritual**] The ancient commentators Aristarchos and Aristophanes suggested that
this was the last line of the *Odyssey* – and they have been supported by many subsequent scholars. There are two central arguments] (1) the alleged redundancy of the rest of the poem; and
(2) its alleged linguistic and stylistic differences. The linguistic and stylistic differences have been
discussed by Page (1955), among others; anyone who has read the poem (even in translation) is
qualified to make their own judgment on whether the rest of the poem is redundant: is this an
effective place to stop the narrative?

310 **beaten the Kikonians**] Odysseus forgets to mention that the Kikonians eventually defeat
him and his men (IX.47–61).

320 This line does not appear in any early manuscripts, and has probably been added to the
poem at a later stage.

He told how he had heard the song of the echoing Sirens,
and made his way to the Roving Rocks and dreaded Charybdis
and Skylla, whom no men ever yet have escaped without damage.
He told how his companions ate the cattle of Helios,
then told how Zeus who thunders on high had struck his fast ship   330
with the smoky thunderbolt, and all his noble companions
perished alike, only he escaped the evil death spirits;
and how he came to the island Ogygia and the nymph Kalypso
who detained him with her, desiring that he should be her husband,
in her hollow caverns, and she took care of him and told him   335
that she would make him ageless all his days, and immortal,
but never so could she persuade the heart that was in him;
then how, after much suffering, he reached the Phaiakians,
who honored him in their hearts as if he were a god, and sent him
back, by ship, to the beloved land of his fathers,   340
bestowing bronze and gold in abundance on him, and clothing.
And this was the last word he spoke to her, when the sweet sleep
came to relax his limbs* and slip the cares from his spirit.
    Then the goddess gray-eyed Athene thought what to do next.
As soon as she thought the heart of Odysseus had full contentment   345
of the pleasure of resting in bed beside his wife, and of sleeping,
immediately she stirred from Ocean the gold-throned early
Dawn, to shine her light upon men, and Odysseus rose up
from his soft bed, and spoke then to his wife, telling her:
'Dear wife, we have had our share of numerous trials   350
now; yours have been here as you cried over my much-longed for
homecoming, while as for me, Zeus and the other gods held me
back from my own country, as I was striving to reach it.
But now that we two have come to our desired bed together,
you look after my possessions which are in the palace,   355
but as for my flocks, which the overbearing suitors have ruined,
many I shall restore by raiding, others the Achaians
shall give me, until they have filled up all of my sheepfolds.
But now I shall go to our estate with its many orchards,
to see my noble father who has grieved for me constantly.   360
But I tell you this, my wife, though you have your own
    understanding.
Presently, when the sun rises, there will be a rumor
about the men who courted you, whom I killed in our palace.
Then go to the upper chamber with your attendant women,
and sit still, looking at no one, and do not ask any questions.'   365

342–3 the sweet sleep / came to relax his limbs] A neat touch. Odysseus falls asleep at the same point in his retelling that he did in his travels.

He spoke, and put his splendid armor over his shoulders,
and wakened Telemachos and the oxherd and the swineherd,
and told all to take up in their hands their warlike weapons;
nor did they disobey him, but armed themselves in the bronze, then
opened the doors and went outside, and Odysseus led them.   370
By now the light was over the earth, but Athene, hiding
these men in darkness, guided them quickly out of the city.

Chapter 4

Contexts for Reading

Oral Poetry and the Homeric Question

For us, the *Odyssey* is a written text – but it is important to bear in mind that it has its origins in a tradition of oral poetry. If we ignore this fact, many of its most prominent features can strike us as merely odd. Why, for example, is there so much repetition in the text? Sometimes noun-epithet combinations are repeated ('wily Odysseus', 'circumspect Penelope', 'the wine-blue sea'), sometimes whole lines ('But when the young Dawn showed again with her rosy fingers'), sometimes substantial passages (such as the description of ritual eating at I.36–40, reproduced at five subsequent points in the poem). The opening lines of speeches, in particular, are often duplicated (I.44–5 = I.80–1, for example). And the use of epithets more generally can be offputting: why does Nausikaa take 'shining' clothes to be washed at VI.26? Why do the suitors (who want Telemachos dead) describe him as 'brilliant' at XIX.21? Why does the beautiful Penelope grasp something in her 'solid hand' at XXI.6? (Lattimore's translation softens the strangeness, the Greek word *pakhei* is more accurately translated as 'fat'.)

Besides these oddities, apparent to any first-time reader of the poem, there are others which baffle scholars of Greek literature and culture. Writing began in Greece at some point after 750 BC, and the Homeric poems can be dated to roughly the same period. How is it possible that a society only just beginning to get to grips with an alphabet (adapted from that of the Phoenicians) could produce poems of such complexity and length? It is, one scholar has written, 'like opening the caves at Lascaux and discovering the Sistine Chapel ceiling inside' (Davidson 1997: 3). Also, when we try to determine the date at which the poems are set, we notice something still stranger. There are references to practices, customs and artefacts from the eighth century BC (such as the building of temples), and from as long ago as the fifteenth (such as the bronze-and-silver sword, with which Odysseus is presented at VIII.406). In the *Iliad*, organised modern practices of warfare ('hoplite practices') co-exist with earlier accounts of duelling noblemen (see Sherratt 1990). The language of the poems, too, is a hybrid; verbal forms from different historical periods come together in a single text (see West 1988). The language of the *Iliad* and the *Odyssey* has been described as *Kunstsprache* – that is to say, a language that only exists in poetry: no-one ever spoke 'Homeric Greek'.

There have been various responses to these difficulties, often referred to collectively as the 'Homeric Question' – and a brief history of critical responses to Homer is attempted below – but the research which caused the most significant shift in our understanding of the poet was conducted in the 1920s by the American scholar Milman Parry. Parry's working thesis was that the oddities in the Homeric poems might be attributed to its origins in an oral tradition. In order to understand the mechanics of a living oral tradition, he put on Serbian national costume, and went out to Yugoslavia where illiterate *guslars* still composed and performed heroic verse. His transcription and analysis of these Slavic poems showed that their singers used a system of 'formulae' in order to allow them to compose in performance. Parry described a formula as 'an expression regularly used, under the same metrical conditions, to express an essential idea' (Parry 1971: 272). His findings are most clearly explained as they relate to fixed epithets.

As we have seen, the Homeric hexameter verse is always essentially the same shape, although it allows space for a certain amount of flexibility. The particular challenge for a poet composing an epic in front of an audience is to find – before he runs out of time – a means of saying what he wants to say which will fit into the hexameter. Fixed formulae – ready-made verbal building blocks – help him to do this. For example, because Odysseus is so frequently mentioned in the poem, it is convenient to be able to make his name occupy spaces of various length, occurring at various different metrical positions. So he has several different epithets, each of which combines with his name to form a metrically distinct formula. The poet's decision at a particular moment to make him *dios Odusseus* (godlike Odysseus) rather than *ptoliporthos* (city-sacking), or *polutlas* (much suffering), or *polutropos* (of many ways) is not dictated by the appropriateness of the epithet but by the size of the gap he has to fill. This is why epithets can sometimes seem – to our minds – perverse. Nausikaa's dirty clothes are 'shining' simply because *sigaloenta* is part of a fixed formula. The suitors call Telemachos 'brilliant' for the same reason. Penelope has a 'fat hand' because the words belong together.

Parry's theory also explains the prominence of repetition in the *Odyssey*. Repeated verses (and groups of verses) allow the poet space to think and to improvise. Repeated preambles occur with particular frequency at the start of speeches because they buy him time at a point when time is particularly welcome. Besides this, thinking of the *Odyssey* as the product of formulaic composition helps to resolve some of the linguistic and archaeological inconsistencies. Archaic verbal forms and outmoded artefacts (which often, of course, coincide) can be seen as having survived in oral formula, developed over the course of several generations.

But Parry's theory, even if we accept it unreservedly (which not all scholars do), does not provide a comprehensive answer to the 'Homeric Question'. The poems may be the product of an oral culture, improvised and developed using traditional formulae – but this doesn't explain how they came to be written documents. There are three possibilities, none of them entirely satisfactory. First, the form of the *Odyssey* could have become settled around the end of the eighth century, and the fixed version dictated many years subsequently (see Kirk 1976: 113–28). We can assume that the text did not continue to evolve beyond this date, as the seventh century has left no linguistic or cultural traces in the text (Janko 1982, though Nagy 1996 argues against this). Second, someone could have transcribed the poem as it was simultaneously composed and performed (an 'oral-dictated text'). In this event, what we have would be a single snapshot of a still-fluid text (see Janko 1998). Or, finally, it could have been written down by a poet schooled in the oral tradition, but who had become literate. The first of these options presumes that an oral text can both acquire and retain total fixity over time, which seems implausible (see Parry 1989). The arrival of an alphabet in late eighth-century Greece makes the other two options more likely – but each of them still requires a leap of faith. For the *Odyssey* to have come into our possession, something extraordinary must have happened, prompted by a collision of oral and literate cultures (whether within a single poet or amongst a society; whether at a single moment, or over the course of several decades). And even these three hypotheses cannot adequately express the range of possibilities. We do not know to what extent the poet drew on his memory of pre-existing material for each new performance, and to what extent he was improvising afresh. At one extreme, we can see him as gradually refining an existing song; at another, as continually composing a new one, repositioning the building

blocks inherited from his predecessors. Besides this, we might entertain
the idea that knowledge of (or contact with) writing allowed the poet
to develop his work to a greater level than would otherwise have been
possible – though it seems to me that this view is born out of mere preju-
dice against oral poetry. (Indeed, Parry insisted that literacy irreparably
damaged an oral poet's ability to improvise.)

The formulaic approach to Homeric epic is susceptible to challenge.
The main objection is that Parry and his followers have been too quick
to see formulae where none exist (for a good summary of the arguments
see Silk 2004: 14–24). Furthermore, by reducing Homeric poetry to a
series of building blocks they have placed too much emphasis on the
mechanical process by which the poems were formed, and diminished
the creative role of the poet (or poets) working within the system. This
seems wrong – when we read, or hear, the *Odyssey* we do not get the
impression that it is a poem simply assembled from a kit, nor that its
repetitions are purely random. Consider, to give one example, the following lines from Odysseus' account of his arrival in the land of the
Lotus-Eaters:

> But after we had tasted food and drink, then I sent
> some of my companions ahead, telling them to find out
> what men, eaters of bread, might live here in this country. (IX.87–9)

The second two lines are repeated verbatim later in Odysseus' account
(at X.100–1), when the Ithakans have arrived in the land of the man-
eating Laistrygones. The echo is significant, because it again shows
Odysseus approaching a strange people with a particular set of cultural
assumptions – and when we encounter it for the second time it comes
freighted with irony and foreboding. We can ascribe this to blind
chance, or to a poet capable of manipulating 'epic formulae' with skill,
thought and some degree of premeditation.

What is now beyond serious doubt is that the traces of a mnemonic
system survive in, and colour, our written text. We can also safely
assume that the poem we have was designed to be *heard* rather than
read. The *Odyssey* itself gives us a glimpse of the kind of environment
in which it might have been heard; in a hall, after a feast, accompanied
by the lyre. Demodokos, the Phaiakian bard, sings in Book VIII about
the Trojan War and the quarrel between Achilles and Odysseus (which
makes Odysseus weep), and later about the love of Ares and Aphrodite
and the Wooden Horse. Phemios in Book I sings of 'the sad return of
the Danaans' (350) – which, equally, Penelope cannot bear to hear.
Reference to these quasi-Homeric songs is intended to impress on the

listener the beauty and importance of the poet's art; Demodokos has often been taken to be a self-portrait – and is probably the origin of the tradition that Homer was blind. The songs within the *Odyssey* should also alert us to the fact that there were other versions of the poem. Some of these versions may exert a ghostly presence in our text (see Griffin 2004: 24–30), but they are largely lost. There is no reference to writing in the *Odyssey*, whose characters we can safely assume to be illiterate (or, rather, pre-literate). The same is true for the characters in the *Iliad*, although there is a reference to the written word in that poem. The Trojan warrior Glaukos tells the Greek Diomedes the story of his grandfather, Bellerophon, who unwittingly carried his own death warrant to the king of Lykia.

> He shrank from killing him, since his heart was awed by such action,
> but sent him away to Lykia, and handed him murderous symbols,
> which he inscribed in a folding tablet, enough to destroy life,
> and told him to show it to his wife's father, that he might perish
>   (VI.167–70)

Here words are dangerous and alien things: murderous symbols (*sēmata*, rather than the usual Greek word for writing, *grammata*). Neither Bellerophon nor Glaukos nor Homer show any understanding of what these markings might be. We don't know how the original audience would have reacted to this embedded story – whether they would have identified with the poem's characters or whether such an attitude to the written word would have appeared quaintly archaic. But the passage highlights the gulf between our world and the world of the Homeric poems – and the challenge we face as readers of this oral text (in whatever way, and to whatever extent that we decide it is oral). There is much in the *Odyssey* that is strange, and this can to some extent be simply ascribed to the circumstances of its composition, and ignored. But alternatively, we might try to appreciate the aesthetic value of this strangeness: the connections highlighted by repeated echoes, the jolts provided by jarring epithets. And this might allow us to approach (without ever exactly nearing) the experience of the poem's first audiences.

Some Views of Homer

Whenever the *Odyssey* was first committed to writing, we know for certain that it was written down by the sixth century BC. The lyric poet Pindar (*c*.518–438 BC) refers to Homer several times by name, and displays an easy familiarity with the content of his poems. In the third and second centuries BC, commentators laboured to establish a definitive text (although even today many lines are still quarrelled over); it may have been during this period that the Homeric poems were each divided into twenty-four books, one for each letter of the Greek alphabet. The best-known commentators were Zenodotos and Aristarchos, who indicated lines which they took to be spurious or corrupt. The most famous example of this was Aristarchos' assertion (still accepted by many scholars) that the true ending of the *Odyssey* comes at XXIII.296 – the moment when Odysseus and Penelope go to bed. The energy expended on the text of Homer indicates what we know from other sources: that he was held in uniquely high regard. This is the case throughout antiquity, from the earliest written texts. Emphasis is placed on his universality, and he is often likened to a spring, or to the ocean. As Dionysius of Halicarnassus puts it (quoting Homer himself, *Iliad* XXI.193–7), he is 'the summit and target of all authors, "from whom all rivers and every sea and all springs . . ."' Heraclitus (writing *c.* AD 100), the proponent of an allegorical approach to the poems, suggested that readers as well as writers owed everything to Homer: 'One might almost say that his poems are our baby clothes, and we nourish our minds by draughts of his milk' (Konstan and Russell 2005: 3).

An influential *negative* view of Homer comes in Plato's *Republic* (written *c.*380 BC), in which Socrates makes Homer the focus of his objections to mimetic art – that is, to art which merely mimics reality. He acknowledges the power of Homer's verse and its ability to move us:

> When even the best of us hear Homer or some other tragedian imitating one of the heroes sorrowing and making a long lamenting speech or singing and beating his breast, you know that we enjoy it, give ourselves up to following it, sympathise with the hero, take his sufferings seriously. (605c–d)

But such engagement is disturbing – both because the emotional behaviour we enjoy in Homer's heroes (Odysseus weeping at the Phaiakian banquet) is exactly the kind of behaviour we should avoid ourselves, and because such accounts are far removed from reality, offering only a feeble imitation of the things described, without inquiring into their true essence. Poets – with Homer as their chief representative – are excluded from Socrates' ideal city (albeit for the dangerous power they hold). Aristotle, writing in *c.*350 BC, is more enthusiastic about the Homeric poems, acknowledging their fundamental place in literary history. He is the first author known to have published a work of Homeric criticism, His major concern in the *Poetics* is tragedy, which he regards as the highest form of mimetic art – but it is worth noting that he, like Socrates, identifies both the *Iliad* and the *Odyssey* as tragic epics. Aristotle also alerts us to the existence of a (now almost entirely lost) comic epic by Homer, the *Margites*. This is almost certainly an error on Aristotle's part – but has been taken as significant by some later interpreters of Homer (see under Reception below).

The nature of Homer and his poems has always been a political issue – never a straightforward matter of disinterested historical enquiry. During the Renaissance, his stock was high. The *Iliad* and *Odyssey* were seen both as the origin and the exemplar of epic poetry. Contained within Homer's poetry (and within that of his most illustrious imitator, Virgil) were the rules to guide future epic poets. Besides this, an allegorical approach meant that the Homeric texts were often taken to provide guidance on matters of faith and kingship (on the Renaissance allegorisation of Homer, see Borris 2000: 13–24). Authors like Edmund Spenser (see also under Literary Responses below) followed ancient commentators in pursuing allegorical readings of the Homeric poems. It was a matter of curiosity, not too deeply probed, that a blind old man, writing at the dawn of history might have produced works far surpassing all that could be written now. There were, it must be acknowledged, dissonant voices; the great humanist scholar Joseph Scaliger (1540–1609) was among those who stressed Homer's inferiority to Virgil – on account of his more primitive nature.

Towards the close of the seventeenth century, opinion began to fragment. First in France, and later in England, there was a clash over the relative merits of ancient and modern learning. The debate covered almost every area of human endeavour (medical science, physics, sculpture), but was most bitterly contested when it came to literature. Indeed, the text which can be said to have initiated the debate was Charles Perrault's *Parallèle des Anciens et des Modernes* (1688–97), in which he pointed out deficiencies in Homer's learning. The 'Battle of the Books', as it became known, followed too convoluted a route to be summarised neatly here (though for a readable account of it see Levine 1991). In a nutshell, the warring factions can be categorised as 'Ancients' – for whom Homer remained an inviolable cultural icon – and Moderns – who thought that the faults in his poems could and should be improved upon. The debate was political, as well as philological; for some 'Ancients' (the satirist Jonathan Swift among them) the attempt to displace Homer was symptomatic of a wider disregard for authority. In 1727, Voltaire offered a fairly conventional (and contemptuous) summary of the 'Ancient' position:

The greatest part of the Critics have fetch'd the rules of *Epick* Poetry from the Books of *Homer*, according to the Custom, or rather, to the Weakness of Men, who mistake commonly the beginning of an Art for the Principles of the Art itself, and are apt to believe, that everything must be by its own Nature, what it was, when contriv'd at first. (*Essay on Epick Poetry*, 1727: 38)

In England the Cambridge classicist Richard Bentley joined Perrault in mocking the idea of Homer's universality, and in suggesting that the poet's intentions were more modest:

Take my word for it, poor *Homer* in those circumstances and early times had never such aspiring thoughts. He wrote a sequel of Songs and Rhapsodies, to be sung by himself for small earnings and good cheer, at Festivals and other days of Merriment; the *Ilias* he made for the men and the *Odysseis* for the other Sex. These loose songs were not connected together in the form of an epic poem till *Pisistratus'* time about 500 years after. (Bentley 1713: 18)

Beyond asserting that Homer was a mere mendicant poet, it is worth noting that Bentley also (on the basis of no external evidence whatever) assumes that the *Odyssey* was written for a female audience; another example of a strong (if misguided) response to the poem's finely-drawn female characters.

Bentley in fact had a great deal of respect for Homer, but insisted on reading him in (what he took to be) his proper historical context. This tactic was also embraced by those who wanted to keep Homer on his pedestal, but needed to explain away the roughness of the people and events he describes. 'What pleases me in the Chinese is Chinese manners,' wrote Anne Dacier, going on, 'If the heroes of Homer's age do not resemble those of our own, that difference should give us pleasure' (quoted in Lane Patey 1997: 57). And this was the general trend of Homeric scholarship in the eighteenth century; there was a growing insistence on seeing Homer as a poet of his own time and culture (whatever that was). Thomas Blackwell's *Enquiry into the Life and Writings of Homer* (1735) again stressed the poet's primitivism, and suggested that readers might admire his poetry, while congratulating themselves on living in the relative comfort of eighteenth-century Britain. Robert Wood's *Essay on the Original Genius of Homer* (1769) was still more historical in approach, illuminating the poems through discussion of topography and archaeology.

The culmination of all these works was F. A. Wolf's *Prolegomena to Homer* (1795), which also drew on a similar trend in German scholarship. Wolf's work revolutionised Homeric scholarship – not least because he was so open about the insoluble nature of the many questions surrounding the *Iliad* and the *Odyssey*. He places great emphasis on the absence of writing from Homer's poems, and argues, glancing back at the theories of Perrault and Bentley, that Homer himself must have been illiterate. He thus identifies the central difficulty, that what we know only as a written text must have its origins in oral poetry. He uses a powerful image to communicate the strangeness of these poems' existence:

> If as the only man of his time to have [pens and a writing tablet] he had completed the *Iliad* and the *Odyssey* in their uninterrupted sequence, they would in their want of all other favorable circumstances have resembled an enormous ship, constructed inland in the first beginnings of navigation: its maker would have had no access to winches and wooden rollers to push it forward, and indeed no access to the sea itself on which to make some trial of his skill. (Wolf [1795] 1985: 116)

An enormous ship miles inland – or a Sistine ceiling in a cave; the difficulties surrounding the Homeric texts endure. Wolf's solution to this intractable problem was to suggest that Homer had composed a series of shorter poems, which were then compiled into our long poem at a later date. (Wolf, like Bentley, thinks this happened in the time of Pisistratus, an Athenian ruler in the sixth century BC; both are leaning on a remark made by Cicero in the first century BC, in his *de Oratore*.)

After Wolf, readers of Homer divided into two camps: 'analysts' and 'unitarians'. Broadly speaking, analysts believed that every inconsistency – or even every problematic moment – in the text could be ascribed to multiple authorship, or to late integration. Typical analytic approaches to the *Odyssey* include the suggestion that the *Telemacheia* is a separate poem, and that the moment in Book XXIII when Odysseus and Penelope go to bed marks the join between two different poems (see Page 1955 for the fullest analyst reading of the poem). Unitarians, in contrast, continued to treat the poems as organic wholes, susceptible to exacting literary criticism, and objected to the idea that the *Iliad* and *Odyssey* are patched together from various songs. For a survey of arguments made by both analysts and unitarians, with particular reference to the proem of the *Odyssey*, see Cook 1995: 15–48.

Our view of Homer changed radically in the 1920s, thanks to Parry's adventures in Yugoslavia and his theory of oral formulae. Once we have acknowledged that the *Iliad* and the *Odyssey* are oral poems, many of the objections posed by the analysts disappear. More than that, the whole starting premise of an analytical approach – the notion that the *Iliad* and the *Odyssey* might have been cobbled together from a number of fixed texts – is exploded. But it is still possible for readers, post-Parry, to have broadly analytic or unitarian viewpoints – and most of them do. An analyst might still seek to show that the work is a collaborative text, produced by the tradition as a whole (Seaford 1994; Nagy 1996), while a unitarian might present an image of a supremely gifted poet, working within that tradition (Taplin 1992).

These are not by any means the only views on the origins of the text, or on the way in which we might approach it; these are too many, and too various, to allow summary here. In general, the past few decades have seen a reaction against the more mechanistic approaches to Homer's verse that have proliferated since Parry's findings were published. Scholars will of course continue to challenge and qualify Parry's theories, and a clearer understanding of the poem's composition and transcription may (or may not) emerge, but readers should not be seduced into allowing the search for origins to determine entirely their approach to the text. Awareness of the *Odyssey*'s oral origins is interesting, and explains many of the poem's oddities, but we must not let this become our sole focus. It is worth bearing in mind that this poem was read, for centuries, by people who had no sense that it might be an oral text – let alone one composed from formulaic building blocks. These people include some of its great imitators, adaptors, and translators – and our understanding of the *Odyssey* is necessarily mediated through what they have written. So, however the landscape of Homeric scholarship may have altered (and may continue to alter), we have an Odyssey which is both oral and written.

The *Odyssey* in English Translation

One gets the impression, glancing at the history of Homeric scholarship, that no two critics ever read the same Homer. The difficulty is exacerbated when we read the *Odyssey* in translation, since someone else has already interpreted the poem for us – and reshaped it according to his or her own ideology. This is, after all, what translators do – whether they admit it or not. Richmond Lattimore's 1965 translation stays close to the Greek (he translates almost line by line – which also makes his version the most useful for students), but it is only one interpretation – which emphasises particular qualities of the poem at the expense of others. Many readers revere Lattimore, but not all of them do; one critic has likened the experience of reading his translation 'to that of some poor rat forced to wade up to the whiskers through an endless morass of chewed tram tickets' (Mason 1972: 201).

The history of Homer in English begins in earnest with George Chapman's translations of the *Iliad* (1598) and *Odyssey* (1614–16), famously celebrated in a sonnet by John Keats (on which, see below); Chapman was the first to translate the poems in their entirety. He rendered the *Iliad* into 'rhymed fourteeners' – which was at that point the usual metre for translations of ancient narrative verse (Arthur Golding's 1564 version of Ovid, Thomas Phaer's 1558–92 Virgil). His *Odyssey*, however, is in 'heroic couplets' – that is to say, rhyming pairs of iambic pentameters. This was to establish itself, over the course of the century, as the standard metre for narrative verse in English. It is not clear whether, or to what extent, Chapman knew Homer in the original Greek (though it seems likely that he leaned heavily on a Latin translation). He frequently omits or alters large sections. But his translation is vivid and fast-paced; the energy of the original survives:

> The man, O Muse, informe, that many a way
> Wound with his wisedome to his wished stay;
> That wanderd wondrous farre when He the towne
> Of sacred Troy had sackt and shiverd downe.
> The cities of a world of nations,
> With all their manners, mindes and fashions
> He saw and knew; at Sea felt many woes,
> Much care sustaind, to save from overthrowes
> Himselfe and friends in their retreat for home.
> But so their fates he could not overcome,
> Though much he thirsted it. O men unwise,
> They perisht by their owne impieties,
> That in their hunger's rapine would not shunne
> The Oxen of the lofty-going Sunne,
> Who therefore from their eyes the day bereft
> Of safe returne. These acts, in some part left,
> Tell us, as others, deified seed of Jove.

As will be clear, Chapman pays great attention to the sound of the verse. He follows Homer in frequent use of enjambment – that is, in allowing his sentences to run on from one line to the next. The energy this gives to his version is evident in the account of Polyphemos' cannibalism:

> He answerd nothing, but rusht in and tooke
> Two of my fellows up from earth and strooke
> Their braines against it. Like two whelps they flew
> About his shoulders, and did all embrew

The blushing earth. No mountaine Lion tore
Two Lambs so sternly . . .

Chapman's principal interest in the *Iliad* was political – as evidenced by his strong identification of Achilles with the troublesome and ultimately rebellious Earl of Essex (out of political expediency Chapman made Achilles a significantly less attractive character in his later books, published after Essex's uprising). The *Odyssey*, by contrast, he treated as a work of sustained moral allegory. Odysseus' journey is, for him (and for countless earlier allegorists on whose work he drew) one which we must all undergo. Translating the passage where we get our first tiny glimpse of the hero, in Athene's description of him languishing on Kalypso's island, Chapman shows us a man whose 'judgment' is pitted against his 'affection'. He justifies the liberty he has taken:

> This is thus translated the rather to expresse and approve the Allegorie driven through the whole Odysses, deciphering the intangling of the Wisest in his affections and the torments that breede in every pious minde: to be thereby hindred to arrive so directly as he desires at the proper and onely true naturall countrie of every worthy man, whose haven is heaven and the next life, to which this life is but a sea, in continuall aesture and vexation. (quoted by Lord 1956: 44)

Chapman's *Odyssey*, as Colin Burrow has argued (1993: 229–33) , is also a mournful work – one which stresses the yearning for a lost past so often encountered in Homer's poem. The most memorable passage, from this point of view, is the four-line passage which Chapman interpolates when commenting on Odysseus' reaction to Demodocus' song in Book VIII.

> In teares his feeling braine swet: for in things
> That move past utterance, teares ope all their springs.
> Nor are there in the Powres that all life beares
> More true interpreters of all than teares.

This lachrymose perspective is an extraordinary, and compelling, one from which to view the poem. The *Odyssey* has been read as a proto-imperialist epic, as a poem dealing with issues of class, race or gender, and as a work of Christian allegory; Chapman's translation also reawakens us to its sadness. The passage is interesting from another point of view, in that Chapman has brought a later text into play while translating Homer (in this case Aeneas' moment of tearfulness at *Aeneid* I.462); this is to become a pattern in subsequent versions.

Less sensitive is the translation of John Ogilby – a prolific writer (Pope was to mock him as 'Ogilby the Great') who published English translations of the complete works of both Homer and Virgil. His *Odyssey* was published in 1665, shortly after the restoration of the monarchy, and is dedicated to James, Duke of Ormonde, a prominent supporter of Charles II (Ogilby's 1660 *Iliad* had been dedicated to the king himself). Ogilby was a fervent Royalist, and his Virgil (1648, revised 1654) was a highly political document, full of not-so-obliquely coded references to the exiled Stuarts. It is tempting to see in his version of the *Odyssey* a celebration of the returning king, reasserting his authority. The heroic couplets of his proem read very differently from his predecessor's; the lack of enjambment between couplets means that it lacks the momentum common to Chapman and Homer:

> What Prudent Heroe's Wandering, Muse, reherse,
> Who (Troy being Sack'd) coasting the Universe,
> Saw many Cities, and their various Modes,
> Much suffering toss'd by Storms on raging Floods,
> His Friends Conducting to their Native Coast;
> But all in vain, for he his Navy lost,
> And they their Lives, prophanely feasting on
> Herds Consecrated to the Glorious Sun;
> Who much incens'd, obstructed so their way,
> They ne're returned: Jove's Daughter this display.

The philosopher Thomas Hobbes turned to Homer in extreme old age; his *Odyssey* was published when he was 87, his *Iliad* a year later. Hobbes's style is strikingly free from elaboration; John Dryden was to describe it, quite reasonably, as 'bald'. Hobbes's version of the proem gives a good indication of his approach:

> Tell me, O Muse, th'Adventures of the Man
>   That having sack'd the sacred Town of Troy,
> Wandred so long at Sea; what course he ran
>   By winds and tempests driven from his way:
> That saw the cities, and the fashions knew
>   Of many men, but suffer'd grievous pain
> To save his own life, and bring home his crew.
>   Though for his crew, all he could do was vain.
> They lost themselves by their own insolence,
>   Feeding, like fools, on the suns sacred Kine.
> Which did the splendid Deity incense
>   To their dire fate. Begin, O Muse divine.*

---

* I have restored the indentations suppressed by Eric Nelson in his edition (Hobbes 2008).

Hobbes had, as the recent editor of his Homeric translations has stressed, a deep-seated suspicion of rhetoric (Hobbes 2008: xxxiii–lv). This dislike of verbal elaboration shines through in his version of the *Odyssey*, both in the straightforward vocabulary he uses himself and in the toning-down or excising of passages in which characters are praised for their rhetoric (one example is *Od*. III.124–5, where Hobbes omits Nestor's kind words about Telemachos' eloquence). Hobbes is offering a poet of an entirely different kind – pitching himself, as Nelson further argues, against those critics who had seen Homer as a semi-divine or prophetic figure. Consequently, he does whatever he can to knock Homer from this pedestal. Whenever a poet or singer is mentioned in either poem, Hobbes tends to downplay their status, describing them as 'minstrels' or 'fidlers'. The alternating rhyme scheme, not usually associated with lofty epic, also has a debunking effect.

Translators of epic characteristically use archaisms and circumlocution in order to preserve the dignity and remoteness of the lofty genre in which they are working. Hobbes does the opposite, always using the simplest word available, and routinely choosing short, Anglo-Saxon-derived words over long, Latinate ones. His account of Polyphemos' man-eating is striking in its directness:

> To this he answer'd nothing, nor said more;
>   But snatching up a couple from the ground,
> Knocks out their brains, like whelps against the floor.
>   Then cuts them into joynts, and on them fed:
> Nor did he flesh, or bone, or entrails leave,
>   Like hungry Lyon on the Mountains bred.

There is much to find fault with in Hobbes's version: awkward shifts in tense, baffling syntax, pointless introduction of ideas not in the original ('then cuts them into joynts'). It does, however, have the virtue of being readily intelligible – far more so than Ogilby's loftier and roughly contemporary translation.

Alexander Pope described Hobbes's translation as 'too mean for criticism'. His own version (1725–6) was written shortly after the success of his version of the *Iliad*. His *Iliad* had been published by subscription between 1715 and 1720, and had made Pope a huge amount of money. Indeed, many critics have taken Pope's Homer as a landmark in the history of publishing: one of the first occasions on which a poet managed to do without patronage, and survive by selling his work directly to the public. To enable him to complete the *Odyssey* more efficiently, Pope enlisted the help of two fellow translators, Elijah Broome and William

Fenton – who between them translated half the poem (Fenton covered Books I, IV, XIX and XX, Broome Books II, VI, VIII, XI, XII, XVI, XVIII and XXIII), Broome also supplying the poem's copious notes. Pope, who could not afford to irritate his subscribers, was deliberately hazy about the mechanics of the group project. But we now know that he operated a system along the lines of a great painter's studio (in which the Master would work on the face and hands of a sitter, leaving his apprentices to paint shadows and folds of cloth). He handled what he considered to be the most important and tricky sections of the poem, and oversaw the whole. Fenton's suggestion for the poem's opening couplet, for example, was,

> The man for wisdom fam'd, O Muse! relate,
> Thro' woes and wanderings long pursu'd by fate

Pope wisely stepped in, and the final version of the proem reads as follows (Fenton's corrected drafts are now in the British Library):

> The Man, for Wisdom's various arts renown'd,
> Long exercis'd in woes, oh Muse! resound.
> Who, when his arms had wrought the destin'd fall
> Of sacred Troy, and raz'd her heav'n built wall,
> Wandring from clime to clime, observant strayed,
> Their Manners noted, and their State survey'd.
> On stormy seas unnumber'd toils he bore,
> Safe with his friends to gain his natal shore:
> Vain toils! their impious folly dar'd to prey
> On Herds devoted to the God of Day;
> The God vindictive doom'd them never more
> (Ah men unbless'd!) to touch that natal shore.
> Oh snatch some portion of these acts from fate,
> Celestial Muse! and to our world relate.

Pope's working methods indicate what big business Homer was in early eighteenth-century England. There was a real desire for a Homer who spoke contemporary English, and this is exactly what Pope and his collaborators supplied. His heroic couplets may sound unduly artificial to a modern ear, and he was accused even in his own time of creating a merely eighteenth-century Homer, with no thought for the increasing emphasis on the poems' historical origins (Richard Bentley is said to have described Pope's *Iliad* as 'a pretty poem, but he must not call it Homer'). But this is unfair: Pope's notes to the *Iliad* show a sustained engagement with recent debates on Homer – as do the notes that Broome supplied for the *Odyssey*. And besides this, his *Iliad* and *Odyssey* are, taken in their entireties, among the great English poems, in which Pope exploits to the full the expressive potential of the heroic couplet – the defining verse form of the period.

Pope is acutely aware of the different – domestic – character of the *Odyssey*, a poem 'not always cloath'd in the majesty of verse proper to Tragedy, but sometimes descends into the plainer Narrative, and sometimes even to that familiar dialogue essential to Comedy' (Pope 1967: 2. 386). Some of the translation's best moments fall in the second half, in descriptions of Ithaka's rugged terrain, and agricultural society. Take this passage, in which Athene describes Eumaios' situation:

> At the *Coracrian* rock he now resides
> Where *Arethusa*'s sable water glides;
> The sable water and the copious mast
> Swell the fat herd; luxuriant, large repaste!
> With him, rest peaceful in the rural cell,
> And all you ask his faithful tongue shall tell.

The passage reads like an excerpt from one of Pope's pastoral poems, and he did not think that it in any way diminished Homer's dignity that he applied his style to matters of this sort; to criticise him for it, he says in his Postscript, 'is to take offence at too much variety'.

Pope's translation was widely read throughout the eighteenth century, but came under challenge towards the end. The high polish of his verse, and the way in which the rhyme scheme dominates the sound of the poem, were seen by many as antithetical to the vision of Homer that had developed over the course of the century (building up to Wolf's *Prolegomena* in 1795). William Cowper wrote that Pope 'who managed the bells of rhyme with more dexterity than any man, tied them about Homer's neck' (*Gentleman's Magazine*, August 1785: 610–13). Cowper's own version, published in 1791, looked to Milton as a model – inspired by his greater freedom.

> Muse make the man thy theme, for shrewdness famed
> And genius versatile, who far and wide
> A Wand'rer, after Ilium overthrown,
> Discover'd various cities, and the mind
> And manners learn'd of men, in lands remote.
> He num'rous woes on Ocean toss'd, endured,
> Anxious to save himself, and to conduct
> His followers to their home. Yet all his care
> Preserv'd them not; they perish'd self-destroy'd
> By their own fault; infatuate! who devour'd
> The oxen of the all-o'erseeing Sun,

And punish'd for that crime, return'd no more.
Daughter divine of Jove, these things record,
As it may please thee, even in our ears.

But although he believes that his freedom from rhyme, and fidelity to the original, gives a clearer sense of Homeric fire, Cowper's version is itself fettered by its tortuous syntax, as in his translation of VI.246–50, when Odysseus is given food by Nausikaa:

Give him, my maidens, food, and give him wine.
She spake; at whose command, her maidens plac'd
With prompt alacrity both wine and food
Before Ulysses; he rapacious ate
And drank with eager lips, for he had liv'd
From taste of aliment long time estranged.

The last line quoted reads like parody of Milton (a danger that Pope had presciently identified in the Postscript to his own translation). The Pope version compares favourably, in terms of the simplicity that both translators value so highly. It also reads better. We might notice that Broome and Pope have retained the near-repetition of the original, where Cowper fussily inverts the words *food* and *wine*:

But haste, the viands and the bowl provide
The maids the viands and the bowl supply'd:
Eager he fed, for keen his hunger rag'd,
And with the generous vintage thirst asswag'd.

The Romantic poets, too, reacted against Pope's Homer – again cherishing an idea of a wild and unfettered genius. John Keats's famous sonnet, 'On First Looking into Chapman's Homer' (1816) describes the thrill he felt on first reading Homer in Chapman's lively and rough-hewn couplets, free from Augustan polish. It is not, as is sometimes thought, a poem about reading Homer for the first time – but about reading Homer unencumbered by Pope; Keats has reached back to a more primitive Homer, and found the experience so refreshing that he reaches for the largest metaphor available: the discovery of a new world:

Much have I travelled in the realms of gold,
And many goodly states and kingdoms seen;
Round many western islands have I been
Which bards in fealty to Apollo hold.
Oft of one wide expanse had I been told
That deep-brow'd Homer ruled as his demesne;
Yet did I never breathe its pure serene
Till I heard Chapman speak out loud and bold:

Then felt I like some watcher of the skies
When a new planet swims into his ken;
Or like stout Cortez when with eagle eyes
He star'd at the Pacific—and all his men
Look'd at each other with a wild surmise—
Silent, upon a peak in Darien. (Keats 1978: 34)

Keats's distaste for an Augustan Homer was to remain the norm for another century (on which see Jenkyns 1980: 192–226). There was a strong tendency for Victorian translators – no doubt influenced by the resurgent interest in ancient British culture – to emphasise the antiquarian, primitive aspect of Homer. William Maginn represented the poems as a series of disconnected ballads (first published between 1838 and 1842, then 1850). P. S. Worsley translated the *Odyssey* into Spenserian stanzas (1861–2). And William Musgrave produced a blank verse version with a distinctly – and explicitly – biblical flavour (1865).

The greatest, and oddest, of the historicising Victorian Homers is that of the pre-Raphaelite William Morris, published in 1887:

Tell me, O Muse, of the Shifty, the man who wandered afar,
After the Holy Burg, Troy-town, he had wasted with war;
He saw the towns of menfolk, and the mind of men he did learn;
As he warded his life in the world, and his fellow-farers' return,
Many a grief of heart on the deep-sea flood he bore,
Nor yet might he save his fellows, for all that he longed for it sore.
They died of their own souls' folly, for witless as they were
They ate up the beasts of the Sun, the Rider of the Air,
And he took away from them all their dear returning day;
O Goddess, O daughter of Zeus, from whencesoever ye may,
Gather the tale, and tell it, yea even to us at the last!

Morris's dislike of Augustanism is well-known. In his translation of the *Aeneid* (1875) he had reached back to the rhymed fourteeners used by the great Tudor translators. For his *Odyssey*, he reaches back further still – or rather, he comes up with a composite verse form which might belong to a yet more distant age (and which he had already used for *The Story of Sigurd*, the pseudo-Icelandic saga he published in 1876): rhyming, loosely anapaestic lines. It suited Morris, who claimed to dislike 'all Classical art and literature' (quoted in McCarthy 1994: 564), to find in Homer something more raw and primitive. He avoids Latinisms, and rejects shop-worn epithets. Thus, whereas Pope translates *polutropos* as 'the man for wisdom's various arts renown'd', Morris gives simply 'the Shifty'. And rather than simply transliterating names, or giving Latinised versions, Morris delves into their etymology and comes up with an Anglo-Saxon equivalent. Thus, in the passage quoted, the Sun is described as 'The Rider of the Air' (activating the etymological root of Hyperion), and when Athene detains the horses of the dawn in Book XXIII they are not Lampos and Phaethon but 'The Gleamer and the Glitterer'. Oscar Wilde acknowledged in a contemporary review that 'the new spirit added in the transfusion may seem to many far more Norse than Greek' (Faulkner 1973: 303). But he also argues that Morris captures something essential to the poem and its language: its stateliness and its strangeness.

An earlier archaising translation of Homer had prompted a famous response from Matthew Arnold. In 1856, F. W. Newman had translated the *Iliad* into something that he hoped sounded like Anglo-Saxon verse – Homer being, he wrote, 'the poet of a barbarian age'. Like other translators, he sought to cut Homer free from stifling Latinisms: 'the entire dialect of Homer being essentially archaic, that of a translation ought to be as much Saxo-Norman as possible, and owe as little as possible to the elements thrown into our language by classical learning' (quoted in Arnold 1960: 100). It was in response to Newman's version, to which Arnold strongly objected, that he issued a famous set of rules on translating Homer. For Arnold, Homer had four essential characteristics, which any translator must keep continually in view:

> that he is eminently rapid; that he is eminently plain and direct both in the evolution of his thought and in the expression of it, that is, both in his syntax and in his words; that he is eminently plain and direct in the substance of his thought, that is, in his matter and ideas; and, finally, that he is eminently noble. (Arnold 1960: 102)

It hardly needs arguing that none of the Victorian versions of the *Odyssey* match Arnold's criteria (though he is curiously tolerant of Worsley's Spenserian version); Arnold's own translations from the *Iliad* were in quantitative hexameters, which fail to capture the 'rapidity' he admired in Homer.

The most plain and direct version of the nineteenth century was the widely circulated prose version of S. H. Butcher and A. Lang (1879). They suggested, like Musgrave, that the language of the King James Bible was analogous to that of the Homeric poems, largely because it is 'a thing of slow growth and composite nature . . . never a spoken language, nor, except for certain poetical purposes, a written language' (ix).

> Tell me, Muse, of that man, so ready at need, who wandered far and wide, after he had sacked the sacred citadel of Troy, and many were the men

whose towns he saw and whose mind he learnt, yea, and many the woes he suffered in his heart on the deep, striving to win his own life and the return of his company. Nay, but even so he saved not his company, though he desired it sore. For through the blindness of their own hearts they perished, fools, who devoured the oxen of Helios Hyperion: but the god took from them their day of returning. Of these things, goddess, daughter of Zeus, whencesoever thou hast heard thereof, declare thou even unto us. (Butcher and Lang 1879: 1)

The Victorian view of Homer was of a virtuous and manly poet. Matthew Arnold's father – Dr Thomas Arnold, the Headmaster of Rugby School – put Homer at the centre of his curriculum because his heroes 'exemplified ideals of masculinity on which his pupils could model their conduct' (Hurst 2006: 19) This is what made the intervention of Samuel Butler so profoundly shocking. Butler argued in *The Authoress of the Odyssey* (1897) that the epic was written by a young noblewoman living in Trapani, Sicily, who represented herself in the poem as Nausikaa. His reasoning was not only that the writer of the *Odyssey* gives unusual prominence to its female characters but also that Book VI is the liveliest and most involved section of the poem:

No one else is drawn with like livingness and enthusiasm, and no other episode is written with the same, or nearly the same, buoyancy of spirits and resiliency of pulse and movement, or brings the scene before us with anything approaching the same freshness, as that in which Nausicaa takes the family linen to, the washing cisterns. (Butler 1897: 201)

Butler attempted to capture that freshness in his 1900 translation:

Tell me, oh Muse, of that ingenious hero who travelled far and wide after he had sacked the famous town of Troy. Many cities did he visit, and many were the nations with whose manners and customs he was acquainted; moreover he suffered much by sea while trying to save his own life and bring his men safely home; but do what he might he could not save his men, for they perished through their own folly in eating the cattle of the Sun-god Hyperion; so the god prevented them from ever reaching home. Tell me, too, about all these things, oh daughter of Jove, from whatsoever source you may know them.

Butler's more colloquial prose suggests the influence of another form: the novel. In the twentieth century, the *Odyssey* was increasingly (and to a far greater extent than the *Iliad*) identified as a novelistic poem. As Butler himself put it, 'The *Odyssey* is not a poem, it is a novel. It was only written in metre because everything that was written at all was in those days written in metre (Butler 1934: 286) (Butler's own version had a strong influence on James Joyce's *Ulysses*; see Kenner 1972: 46–50). In his note books, Butler wrote of the importance he attached to the use of everyday language:

> Whenever this is attempted, great licence must be allowed to the translator in getting rid of all those poetical common forms which are foreign to the genius of prose. If the work be translated into prose, let it be into such prose as we write and speak among ourselves. (Butler 1917: 197)

In a neat parallel – and as if to suggest further that the forms of epic and novel were interchangeable – he also rendered a famous passage of Dickens (Mrs Gamp's speech in *Martin Chuzzlewit*) into Greek hexameters (Butler 1917: 393).

T. E. Lawrence (better known as 'Lawrence of Arabia') produced in 1932 a prose translation which continued the trend of 'novelising' the poem. Like Butler, Lawrence believed firmly that the *Odyssey* was the later production of a very different poet, and his translation is informed by this belief. He writes in his preface that the *Odyssey* is 'crafty' and 'exquisite' narrative:

> In this tale every big situation is burked and the writing is soft. The shattered *Iliad* yet makes a masterpiece; while the *Odyssey* by its ease and interest remains the oldest book worth reading for its story and the first novel of Europe. (Lawrence 1932: preface)

Lawrence has the proem printed like a monumental inscription:

O DIVINE POESY
GODDESS DAUGHTER OF ZEUS
SUSTAIN FOR ME
THE SONG OF THE VARIOUS-MINDED MAN
WHO AFTER HE HAD PLUNDERED
THE INNERMOST CITADEL OF HALLOWED TROY
WAS MADE TO STRAY GRIEVOUSLY
ABOUT THE COASTS OF MEN
THE SPORT OF THEIR CUSTOMS GOOD OR BAD
WHILE HIS HEART
THROUGH ALL THE SEA-FARING
ACHED IN AN AGONY TO REDEEM HIMSELF
AND BRING HIS COMPANY STRAIGHT HOME

VAIN HOPE – FOR THEM
FOR HIS FELLOWS HE STROVE IN VAIN
THEIR OWN WITLESSNESS CAST THEM AWAY
THE FOOLS
TO DESTROY FOR MEAT

THE OXEN OF THE MOST EXALTED SUN
WHEREFORE THE SUN-GOD BLOTTED OUT
THE DAY OF THEIR RETURN

MAKE THE TALE LIVE FOR US
IN ALL ITS MANY BEARINGS
O MUSE

Lawrence makes the tale 'live' by casting it into idiomatic, and occasionally eccentric, prose: 'By now the other warriors, those that had escaped headlong ruin by sea or in battle, were safely home. Only Odysseus tarried, shut up by Lady Calypso, a nymph and very Goddess, in her hewn-out caves.' He has a taste for archaism, which renders his prose rather stilted – but the translation is energetic, and paves the way for the prose versions of the later twentieth century.

The most significant of these (though not necessarily the most successful), is that of E. V. Rieu, published in 1946 – just after servicemen across Europe had returned to their wives. Rieu follows Lawrence and Butler in suggesting that the *Odyssey*, 'with its well-knit plot, its psychological interest and its interplay of character, is the true ancestor of the long line of novels which have followed it' (Rieu 1946: viii). Like Lawrence, he seems a little embarrassed by the proem – which forces us to confront the orality of the *Odyssey*, the fact that it is a poem, or song – and prints it in italics as a mere prelude to his prose narrative. It is worth noticing that he has suppressed all words related to singing (though his translation has its origins in oral performance, of a sort; he first translated the poem in order to read it to his wife):

> *The hero of the tale which I beg the Muse to help me tell is that resourceful man who roamed the wide world after he had sacked the holy citadel of Troy. He saw the cities of many peoples and he learnt their ways. He suffered many hardships on the high seas in his struggles to preserve his life and bring his comrades home. But he failed to save those comrades, in spite of all his efforts. It was their own sin that brought them to their doom, for in their folly they devoured the oxen of Hyperion the Sun, and the god saw to it that they should never return. This is the tale I pray to the divine Muse to unfold to us. Begin it, goddess, at whatever point you will.*

Rieu's translation has been, in its own way, as influential as those of Chapman and Pope – and not only because of its massive sales (Penguin has sold well over three million copies). It was published as the inaugural volume in the Penguin Classics series. Rieu himself was the general editor of Penguin Classics until 1964, and intended his *Odyssey* to serve as an example of good practice to the translators he commissioned; he wanted them to write intelligible, colloquial English, and frequently commissioned translations from novelists – Robert Graves and Dorothy L. Sayers among them – rather than academics (see Hare 2008). Some readers have found Rieu's easy style unpalatable. When Zeus chastises Athene for questioning his treatment of Odysseus, Lattimore (sticking fairly close to the Greek) has him say: 'My child, what sort of word escaped your teeth's barrier?' Rieu gives: 'Nonsense, my child!' And he regularly omits or elides the traditional epithets by which characters are addressed.

Parry's findings on Homeric formulae and his theory of oral composition seem to have had little impact on Rieu's translation. Rieu shies away from the traces of orality at every opportunity. For this reason, perhaps, his severest critic was Parry's son, Adam, himself a distinguished classicist, who held his novelised version of the *Odyssey* in contempt: 'Rieu was the first to demonstrate beyond a doubt that Homer was really Anthony Trollope' (Parry 1989: 42).

There has been, since the 1940s, a renewed interest in reading the *Odyssey* as a poem (although the popularity of Rieu's translation persisted, and further prose versions have appeared – most notably Walter Shewring's in 1980). In 1961, Robert Fitzgerald produced a translation which stressed the oral origins of the verse, and presented the poet as a vehicle through whom the Muse can sing. The metre is – for the most part – iambic pentameter. There are a good deal of shorter lines, however, and Fitzgerald is bold about rearranging the stress; *after he plundered the stronghold*, for example, is almost entirely dactylic. These metrical shifts are unassuming, and the result comes close to satisfying Arnold's criteria of rapidity and plainness:

> Sing in me, Muse, and through me tell the story
> of that man skilled in all ways of contending,
> the wanderer, harried for years on end,
> after he plundered the stronghold
> on the proud height of Troy.
>
>   He saw the townlands
> and learned the minds of many distant men,
> and weathered many bitter nights and days
> in his deep heart at sea, while he fought only
> to save his life, to bring his shipmates home.
> But not by will nor valor could he save them,
> for their own recklessness destroyed them all –
> children and fools, they killed and feasted on
> the cattle of Lord Hêlios, the Sun,

and he who moves all day through heaven
took from their eyes the dawn of their return.

Of these adventures, Muse, daughter of Zeus,
tell us in our time, lift the great song again.

Fitzgerald's translation remains, like most of its predecessors, solemn; he has a gift for breathing fresh life into Homeric turns of phrase (for example, his Polyphemos calls Odysseus 'small, pitiful and twiggy' where Lattimore gives 'a little man, niddering, feeble' IX.515) but his diction remains self-consciously archaic. Some of that solemnity is shaken off in Stanley Lombardo's 2000 version:

SPEAK, MEMORY –

                      Of the cunning hero,
The wanderer, blown off course time and again
After he plundered Troy's sacred heights.

                           Speak
Of all the cities he saw, the minds he grasped,
The suffering deep in his heart at sea
As he struggled to survive and bring his men home
But could not save them, hard as he tried –
The fools – destroyed by their own recklessness
When they ate the oxen of Hyperion the Sun,
And that god snuffed out the day of their return.

                      Of these things,
Speak, Immortal One,
And tell the tale once more in our time. (Lombardo 2000: 1)

Again, the poem's oral origins are stressed. But Lombardo goes further than most of his predecessors in the extent to which he is prepared to modernise. For him, to 'tell the tale once more in our own time' is to pepper it with twentieth-century colloquialisms; 'snuffed out' is only the first of hundreds – perhaps the most striking one occurring when Melanthios calls the disguised Odysseus a 'walking pile of shit'. One might argue that to have everyday words and earthy language rubbing up against the elements of epic diction is as true as any earlier translation to the spirit of the original.

Literary Responses

Quite apart from attracting the attention of critics and translators, the *Odyssey* has had a busy afterlife in original works by countless novelists, playwrights and poets. Its reception has been extraordinarily varied – reflecting the poem's own heterogeneity and richness. There is insufficient space here to cover in full the many literary responses to the poem. For a fuller account, see Stanford (1954), Hall (2008), and many of the essays collected by Fowler (2005), and Graziosi and Greenwood (2007). In this survey, I focus on two overlapping areas: the role of the *Odyssey* in the development of epic poetry, and the influence the poem has had on prose fiction.

The *Odyssey* and Epic Poetry

Epic continued to be written in Greece after Homer, but there are few surviving examples. We therefore have a false sense of the *Iliad* and the *Odyssey*'s singularity; it may be reasonable to regard them as singular in terms of their character and quality, but we should remember that they were two poems among many. In the sixth century, Homer's epics would have been known as part of an 'epic cycle' alongside other poems (probably written slightly later). We know the names of these other epics, and can guess at their content, but they are lost. Later epic poems do survive. Perhaps the most engaging of these is Apollonius of Rhodes' *Argonautica* (composed around the middle of the third century BC), an epic poem in four books telling the story of Jason and the Argonauts, and their quest to recover the golden fleece. The subject matter of this poem invites parallels with the *Odyssey*, and Homer's constant presence in the texture of Apollonius' verse gives an indication of the esteem in which he was already held.

One of the earliest Roman epics – indeed, one of the foundational works of Latin literature – is a translation of the *Odyssey* by Livius Andronicus, composed in the second half of the third century BC. The Romans, despite having conquered Greece in 146 BC, continued to feel an overwhelming sense of anxiety in the face of Greek culture, and this was nowhere more evident than in their veneration of Homer. Ennius (239–169 BC), often credited as the father of Roman epic, wrote a historical epic in hexameters, the *Annales* (like Livius' *Odyssey*, this survives only in fragments). The poem opens with a dream sequence in which Homer himself appears, and announces that his spirit lives on in Ennius. It is the much later poet Virgil (70–19 BC) who is now regarded as the Roman Homer. Virgil seems to have seen himself as competing with Homer, rather than merely reviving his spirit. The twelve books of the *Aeneid* aim to compress the subject matter of the forty-eight books of Homer, as is clear from the opening words, 'I sing of arms and the man' (*arma uirumque cano* – *arma* is usually taken to allude to the subject matter of the *Iliad*, and *uirum*, 'man', to that of the *Odyssey*). The first half of the *Aeneid* is broadly Odyssean, charting the journey of the Trojan prince Aeneas after the fall of Troy. A large section of this narrative (Books II–III) is told in the first person, as Aeneas addresses the Carthaginian court after a banquet (corresponding to Odysseus' narration in *Odyssey* IX–XII). Aeneas' visit to the underworld in *Aeneid* VI corresponds to that undertaken in *Odyssey* XI. And as is the case with Odysseus, there are many people and things which threaten to detain him – most notably the beguiling Dido, an amalgam of Circe, Kalypso and Nausikaa. The chief difference is that, while Odysseus is motivated by a desire to see his homeland, his wife and his son, Aeneas is forced to forget his homeland and to pursue an imperial mission. He is instead commanded by the gods to travel to Italy and found a new settlement, which will ultimately become Rome. Readers have been divided as to whether the resulting poem is a expression of hard-nosed patriotism or a study of the human cost of empire-building. The second half of the *Aeneid* (in which Aeneas battles with indigenous Etruscans in order to win the hand of the princess Lavinia) has usually been seen as Iliadic, but there is also much about it that is Odyssean – not least the poem's ending, which promises a symbolic union and a restored political settlement.

The *Odyssey* exerts a shadowy presence in the epic poetry of the Middle Ages and Renaissance. Dante, for example, did not have access to the text of Homer, but is happy to hail him as the *poeta sovrano* or 'supreme poet' at *Inferno* IV.88). The descent to the underworld which makes up the first part of *The Divine Comedy* (1307–21) relies heavily on *Aeneid* VI, which is in turn influenced by *Odyssey* XI. Ariosto *might* have read Homer in a Latin translation – but it is equally possible that his knowledge of the text was mediated through other sources. In either case, his *Orlando Furioso* (final version 1532) has much in common with the *Odyssey*: the wanderings of its hero, Ruggiero, its fairytale atmosphere, the prominence it gives to internal narrators – not to mention the reworked similes and battle scenes.

English epic of the early Renaissance is more often Virgilian than Homeric. This is certainly true of Edmund Spenser, though he shows a detailed knowledge of the *Odyssey* in Book II, Canto XII of *The Faerie Queene* (1590–6), where he offers a miniaturised version of Odysseus' travels. There we see the hero Guyon voyage through a sea that teems with dangerous temptations: the *Gulfe of Greedinesse*, the *Rock of Reproch*, the *Whirlpool of Decay* and so on. These reflect the longstanding tradition of allegorising the trials of Odysseus – and the presentation of the trials in exactly forty stanzas (a number associated with the temptation of Christ) suggests an attempt to assimilate the poem's Homeric and Christian heritage. A more thorough-going engagement with the *Odyssey* comes in John Milton's *Paradise Lost* (1667). Like Virgil before him, Milton felt a duty not just to imitate but to surpass Homer – in this case because of the superior nature of his subject matter: the fall of man. *Paradise Lost* opens, like the *Odyssey* and the *Aeneid*, with a promise to sing of a man:

> Of man's first disobedience, and the fruit
> Of that forbidden tree, whose mortal taste
> Brought death into our world, and all our woe,
> With loss of Eden, till one greater man
> Restore us, and regain the blissful seat,
> Sing heavenly Muse (I.1–6)

But while the *Odyssey* is concerned with the adventures of a single man, Milton's man stands for all mankind. More than that, he (Adam) is the precursor to a 'greater man' (Christ) who will atone for his original sin. And it is Satan who is more frequently identified with Odysseus (and other pagan heroes), as when he undertakes his flight to Paradise, 'harder beset / And more endangered, than when Argo passed / Through Bosporus betwixt the jostling rocks: / Or when Ulysses on the larboard shunned / Charybdis, and by the other whirlpool steered' (II.1016–20). The characters in Milton's poem aspire to a different kind of heroism. One important way in which Milton reaches back to Homer – for all his efforts to transcend him – is in his choice of metre: blank verse, with frequent enjambment, rhyme being 'the invention of a barbarous age' (Milton here activates the etymology of barbarous, which derives from the Greek word *barbaros*, meaning 'one who cannot speak Greek').

The *Odyssey* has provided, as I will discuss below, the template for many modern novels. This must – at least in part – be due to its heterogeneous and earthy feel; its characters are drawn from across the social spectrum, and exist in a world of swineherds and cauldrons as well as warring princes. The poem has also inspired responses which stress its earthy qualities while remaining firmly within the epic tradition. This is the case with Nikos Kazantzakis's *Odyseia* (1938, translated into English hexameters by Kimon Friar as *The Odyssey: A Modern Sequel* in 1958). In Kazantzakis's epic, Odysseus is a restless wanderer (Tennyson perceived him similarly in his 1833 poem, 'Ulysses') who resolves to leave Ithaka for good immediately after he has killed the suitors. Kazantzakis may have taken a hint from Teiresias' words to Odysseus at *Odyssey* XI.120–4:

> But after you have killed these suitors in your own palace,
> either by treachery, or openly with the sharp bronze,
> then you must take your well-shaped oar and go on a journey
> until you come to where there are men living who know nothing of the
>   sea

The *Odyseia* picks up from this speech, opening 'And when in his wide courtyards Odysseus had cut down / the insolent youths ... ' His subsequent journey takes him first to Sparta (where he abducts Helen), and then on to Crete, Egypt and the South Pole. Here, Odysseus dies. While writing the poem, Kazantzakis travelled across Greece, making notes of words and idioms used by peasants in everyday speech but unknown in written Greek (until fairly recently there was a significant gulf between the 'demotic' and the written language); a glossary of around 2,000 words was appended to his *Odyseia*. By plundering the various dialects of Greece for turns of phrase, Kazantzakis had created his own *Kunstsprache*, a language which did not correspond to the native language of any single Greek – and which has no life outside the poem. The oral basis of the *Odyseia* is a fiction, since the poem has never existed in any unwritten form – but it shows a belief that the *Odyssey* belongs in the language of ordinary people, as well as a keen awareness of recent developments in Homeric scholarship.

The most recent installment in the Odyssean epic tradition is Derek Walcott's *Omeros* (1990) – the title is the modern Greek word for Homer. *Omeros* is a narrative poem written in what Walcott himself describes as a 'rough-textured *terza rima*' (that is, the metre of Dante). The narrative shifts between the twentieth and the eighteenth centuries, between the Caribbean, Africa, Britain and the United States. At its core are two groups of characters on St Lucia: Achille and Hector, rivals for the mesmerising Helen; and Major Dennis Plunkett and his wife Maud, childless British settlers. It is Dennis's longing for a son that gives the poem its closest tie to the *Odyssey* (though there are hundreds of local echoes). The narrator makes the parallel explicit after Maud's death, when he encounters

> there in that khaki Ulysses

there was a changing shadow of Telemachus
in me, in his absent war, and an empire's guilt
stitched in the one pattern of Maud's fabulous quilt. (LII.iii)

But quite apart from any structural similarities, *Omeros* follows the *Odyssey* in the largeness of its scope, and in its emphasis on memory and return; Achille dreams of return to Africa, Plunkett has rejected England for the Caribbean, the narrator is torn between Boston and St Lucia. Walcott's poem focuses on the minutiae of everyday life (*Omeros* was described as 'novelistic' by some reviewers), but it also aims at universality. There is a telling passage in which the narrator offers an etymology of Homer's name, having been told it by the Greek expatriate, Antigone:

> I said "Omeros,"
>
> and *O* was the conch-shell's invocation, *mer* was
> both mother and sea in our Antillean patois,
> *os*, a grey bone, and the white surf as it crashes
>
> and spreads its sibilant collar on a lace shore.
> Omeros was the crunch of dry leaves, and the washes
> that echoed from a cave-mouth when the tide has ebbed. (I.iii)

The passage places Homer in the coastal landscape shared by the *Odyssey* and *Omeros* (Walcott has said that '"epic" makes people think of great wars and great warriors. That isn't the Homer I was thinking of; I was thinking of Homer the poet of the seven seas'). The passage also emphasises Homer's orality; he is understood as a succession of sounds. Finally, the play on *mer* glances back to the long-held view of Homer as both universal and fundamental – characterised as both ocean and parent. Towards the end of the poem the narrator (a fictionalised version of Walcott) finally meets Homer, and tells him: 'I have always heard / your voice in that sea, master' (LVI.iii).

This section has dealt only with authors who write in verse and identify themselves (explicitly or otherwise) as epic poets. The *Odyssey*'s influence is perhaps greater still in the field of prose fiction.

The *Odyssey* and the Novel

As we have seen, Samuel Butler, T. E. Lawrence and E. V. Rieu saw the *Odyssey* as the forerunner of the modern novel: 'the first novel of Europe'. There is no doubt that the success of Rieu's prose translation, in particular, rested partly on its resemblance to a novel – both in its workmanlike prose and in its attractive, affordable packaging. The *Odyssey* has in fact had an influence on prose fiction from late antiquity onwards. A number of Greek Romances imitate the poem's structure. One such is Chariton's *Chaereas and Callirhoe*; the narrative features adventures at sea, the separation of a married couple, and a sequence of recognition scenes – and in telling it Chariton quotes around thirty Homeric hexameters. The novel for which the *Odyssey* provides the most important model, though, is the *Aithiopika*, or *Ethiopian Story*, of Heliodorus (date contested, but probably between AD 350 and 375). This is the story of two lovers, Theagenes and Chariclea, who must return (via a suitably circuitous route) to Ethiopia, where Chariclea hopes to be recognised by her father. From the outset, the debt to Homer is clear; a group of Egyptian bandits watch the lovers on a beach, amidst the debris of a violently interrupted banquet – as though we are picking up from the close of the *Odyssey*. Local references abound: most striking are the hunting scar by which Theagenes is identified (Heliodorus 1957: 114) and Odysseus' own appearance to Calasiris in a dream, in which he compares Chariclea to Penelope (128–9). But the clearest debt of all is structural. The reader of the *Aithiopika* is thrown *in medias res*, and the gaps in the narrative are filled by retrospective first-person narration. The narrator in this instance is Kalasiris, who alludes at the outset to his famous predecessor, telling the fellow-diner who asks for his life story: 'you ask an Odyssey' (50). Odysseus is made a prototype for a figure familiar to all readers of novels: the unreliable narrator.

Greek prose fiction tends to concern the chaste adventures of nobly-born young lovers (Theagenes occasionally becomes hot under the collar, but can always be quelled). Roman novels – only two survive, one of which is incomplete – respond to the earthier elements of the *Odyssey*: food and sex are everywhere. The earlier of the survivors is Petronius' *Satyricon* (*c.* AD 65), in which (so far as we can tell from the surviving fragments) the antihero Encolpius is punished for having offended the god Priapus, his punishment being impotence. His subsequent tribulations closely track those that Odysseus undergoes after offending Poseidon. To give one example, Encolpius has abducted a good-looking slaveboy called Giton. When his owner sends someone to find him at the tavern where they are staying,

> I gave the word to Giton to crawl smartly under the bed, to hook his feet and hands into the webbing which lashed the mattress to the bed-frame, and thus to elude prying hands, just as Ulysses of old clung to the ram's belly. (Petronius 1997: 85)

Equally earthy in character is Apuleius' *Metamorphoses*, or *Golden Ass* (*c.* AD 170). This novel is narrated by Lucius, an inquisitive and lustful young man, whose snooping around in the affairs of a witch results in his being transformed into a donkey. There is a clear structural parallel with the *Odyssey*, in that Lucius' wanderings are also a return journey – although in this case the longed-for *nostos* is his regaining human form. There are, again, several allusions and reworkings along the way. One of the most spectacular is the flirtatious stand-off between Lucius and the slavegirl Fotis – written in imitation of Odysseus and Nausikaa's conversation in *Odyssey* VI – which takes place in a kitchen and results in almost immediate sex (for further discussion of this allusion and others, see Harrison 1990).

These Roman authors saw the *Odyssey* as an appropriate template for their seamy stories of lust and appetite, but other writers were to fashion novels after a purer and chaster reading of the poem. One particularly influential work was Fénelon's *Télémaque*, a didactic romance about the pitfalls which faced Odysseus' son – essentially recounting various scenes missing from the *Odyssey*. Its professed purpose was to provide moral instruction for Fénelon's pupil, the grandson of Louis XIV, and it is a book with an unmistakeable seriousness of purpose. Politically engaged as well as morally upright, it firmly rejects the notion of arbitrary government and 'boldly advocates policies of free enterprise and broad religious tolerance' (Beasley 1982: 27). *Télémaque* was extremely popular in England, and went through twenty-five English editions during the first four decades of the eighteenth century – just as the novel was gaining recognition as a literary form. Its influence can be seen in the work of Richardson, Fielding and Smollett – and consequently on later authors who took the moral education of an individual as their subject (Austen and Dickens among them). The *Telemacheia* of the *Odyssey*'s first four books has thus provided the template for a common form of modern narrative: the *Bildungsroman*, or coming-of-age novel.

At least one early English novelist drew inspiration directly from Homer. Henry Fielding's *Tom Jones* ([1749] 2005) is described by its author as belonging to a 'new Species of Writing'. Fielding set out to write a 'comic epic poem in prose', which he believed would fill the gap left by the disappearance of the *Margites*, the comic epic attributed to Homer by Aristotle (see p. 100 above). It is clear that this new species of writing owes a great deal to the *Odyssey*. The epigraph to the novel is taken from Horace's *Ars Poetica*: *mores hominum multorum uidit* ('he saw the customs of many men'), and comes from a passage in which Horace translates the opening lines of the poem in order to praise its structure. Tom, the hero of Fielding's book, is a young man of strong appetites and essential moral goodness who must return home after a series of adventures. He is also a young man who must come of age

(Fielding acknowledges Fénelon as an influence as well). Throughout *Tom Jones* there is fertile tension between the novel's base and lusty elements and its high-flown Homeric model. This tension is enacted on a structural level: Tom spends much of his time pursuing the beautiful Sophia, whose name suggests that she is an embodiment of the wisdom that he needs to acquire (*sophia* is the Greek word for wisdom), but who is also a creature of flesh and blood, to whom Tom is strongly sexually attracted. It is also visible in the novel's language – and particularly, perhaps, in the Fielding's imaginative reworkings of similes, battle scenes and invocations. The play between epic conventions and everyday activities is intended to entertain – but Fielding also uses his Homeric inheritance to elevate the status of his characters, and of the novel itself (at a time when many critics refused to take it seriously as a literary form). It is also worth observing that *Tom Jones* is strongly influenced by the tradition of picaresque fiction, which had flourished in the sixteenth and seventeenth centuries. Picaresque narratives recount the adventures – often strikingly discontinuous – of a *picaro* (the Spanish word means 'rogue'), and often draw heavily on the work of Apuleius, and other ancient novelists (see Sandy and Harrison 2008). Fielding thus owes a triple debt to the *Odyssey*; his novel is shaped by direct reading of the Homeric text, by the tradition of picaresque narrative and by Fénelon's *Télémaque*.

In James Joyce's *Ulysses*, which is explicitly and painstakingly modeled on the *Odyssey*, all of Homer's vast chronological and geographical sweep is compressed into a single city, Dublin, and a single day, 16 June 1904. The Odysseus figure, Leopold Bloom, and the Telemachos figure, Stephen Dedalus (the subject of Joyce's earlier *Bildungsroman*, *A Portrait of the Artist as a Young Man*, 1916) go about their daily business, encountering as they do so various Homeric figures: Polyphemos becomes a boorish drunk in Barry Kiernan's pub, while Nausikaa is represented by the marriage-obsessed Gerty MacDowell. Both Bloom and Dedalus are somewhat in need of redemption, and find it in one another when they meet in a maternity hospital. For all that *Ulysses* is a thorough-going adaptation of Homer's epic, it is also a realistic portrait of modern life – with all its pleasures and indignities. Joyce incorporates a great deal of Edwardian slang and Irish idiom into the work – not to mention excerpts from music hall lyrics, popular journalism, romantic novels and much else besides. These scraps of everyday English sit alongside allusions to, and parodies of, many canonical works of English and European literature. The result is an extraordinary amalgam, and a form of mock-heroic. As with Fielding's mock-heroic, though, the reader is not simply invited to observe the gulf between shabby modernity and the age of heroes. Bloom is elevated by association with Ulysses/Odysseus, whom Joyce significantly described as 'the most human [subject] in world literature' (quoted in Ellman 1959: 430). Odysseus' evident humanity is what makes his journey the perfect template for Bloom's wanderings. It also explains why he has exerted such a strong presence in recent literature. Hall (2008: 52) credits *Ulysses* with prompting 'the flood of updated *Odyssey* plots in the fiction and cinema of the twentieth and twenty-first centuries'.

Chapter 5

Teaching the Text

Each of the five books of the *Odyssey* printed in this guide can provide the starting point for an interesting and diverse seminar or class. In the notes that follow, I suggest ways in which teachers can initiate discussion of the text, and other texts (ancient and modern) to which they might refer. I also make a few suggestions for further reading (but for more information, see under Resources, pp. 137–40). I assume people will have access to a copy of Lattimore's complete translation.

TEACHING BOOK I

Ask students to consider these questions to consider in advance of the seminar

- What is the function of the story of Agamemnon and Aigisthos, told at I.32–43 and 298–300? (You might find it helpful to look also at IV.421–40, XI.404–34, and XXIV.191–202.)
- What is gained (and what is lost) by delaying Odysseus' first appearance for so long? Why does Homer begin the narrative in Ithaka, and at this particular moment – twenty years, that is, after Odysseus' departure for Troy?
- What sort of narrative does the proem lead us to expect? (Those who have already read the *Odyssey* in its entirety might also consider how accurate it is.)
- Why does Athene choose to appear to Telemachos in disguise? Is there any purpose to the lies she tells him?

Seminar activities
Gods and men. Ask students to read lines 64–79, in which we see the gods discussing Odysseus' fate, and to consider the following questions.

To what extent is Odysseus' fate settled at the start of the poem?
How and why do the gods involve themselves in human affairs?
In what ways is their behaviour similar to that of the mortal
characters, and in what ways is it different?

Scholarly stances. Ask students to read lines 271–96, in which Athene
gives Telemachos a series of instructions. Scholars have been divided
by this speech, in which Athene seems to contradict herself. The speech
has even been held up as a central piece of evidence by those critics who
believe that the Homeric poems were stitched together from a number
of smaller works (see Page 1955: 52–64). Split the seminar into two
groups and ask each of them to put one side of the argument – one half
highlighting its inconsistencies, the other half explaining how it fits into
the poem as a whole.

Comparative work: imitating Homer's opening
Ask students to think about the ways in which various epic poets open
their narratives. Printed here are three other epic proems – two serious-
minded, one parodic – each written partially in imitation of Homer
(but each also drawing inspiration from intervening imitators). Divide
students into three groups, and ask each group to look at one of these
passages. They should consider, in particular: what each poet has taken
from Homer and what he has rejected; and how the different proems
indicate different understandings of the value of epic poetry and of
narrative technique.

> I tell about war and the hero who first from Troy's frontier,
> Displaced by destiny, came to the Lavinian shores,
> To Italy – a man much travailed on sea and land
> By the powers above, because of the brooding anger of Juno,
> Suffering much in war until he could found a city
> And march his gods into Latium, whence rose the Latin race,
> The royal line of Alba and the high walls of Rome.
> Where lay the cause of it all? How was her godhead injured?
> What grievance made the queen of heaven so harry a man
> Renowned for piety, through such toils, such a cycle of calamity?
> Can a divine being be so persevering in anger? (Virgil, *Aeneid*,
>   I.1–11, trans. C. Day Lewis (1954))

> Of man's first disobedience, and the fruit
> Of that forbidden tree whose mortal taste
> Brought death into the world, and all our woe,
> With loss of Eden, till one greater man

Restore us, and regain the blissful seat,
Sing heavenly Muse, that on the secret top
Of Oreb, or of Sinai, didst inspire
That shepherd who first taught the chosen seed,
In the beginning how the heavens and earth
Rose out of chaos; or, if Sion hill
Delight thee more, and Siloa's brook that flowed
Fast by the oracle of God, I thence
Invoke thy aid to my adventurous song,
That with no middle flight intends to soar
Above the Aonian mount, while it pursues
Things unattempted yet in prose or rhyme. (John Milton, *Paradise
 Lost* (1667), I.1–16 [in Milton 1998])

What dire offence from amorous causes springs,
What mighty contests rise from trivial things,
I sing – This verse to CARYLL, Muse! is due:
This, even Belinda may vouchsafe to view:
Slight is the subject, but not so the praise,
If She inspire, and He approve my lays.
Say what strange motive, Goddess! could compel
A well-bred lord t'assault a gentle belle?
O say what stranger cause, yet unexplored,
Could make a gentle belle reject a lord?
In tasks so bold can little men engage,
And in soft bosoms dwells such mighty rage? (Alexander Pope, *The
 Rape of the Lock* (1714), I.1–12 [in Pope 1993])

TEACHING BOOK VI

Ask students to consider these questions in advance of the seminar

- Why is marriage mentioned so frequently in this book? Does Homer encourage us to entertain seriously the idea that Nausikaa and Odysseus might get married?
- How does the poet's characterisation of Nausikaa differ from his portrayal of Kalypso or Circe. Also read V.148–224 (Kalypso) and XI.302–409 (Circe), and see Griffin (1980b: 56–62).
- What kind of threat does Nausikaa pose to Odysseus, and vice versa? How does each of them seek to neutralise this threat?
- What shared social and cultural practices underlie the encounter between Odysseus and Nausikaa? (You may want to compare it with that between Odysseus and Polyphemos.)

Seminar activity

Homer's language. Ask students to read closely lines 127–38, in which Odysseus appears on the shore, and to consider: how the lion simile affects the way we view Odysseus? Does the simile clarify or complicate the narrative? Does it coincide with any single character's point of view? Divide them into pairs and ask each pair to choose another simile, from any point in the poem, and identify ways in which it is similar to, or different from, this one.

Comparative work: Rewriting Book VI

Ask students to read, in advance of the seminar, section 13 of James Joyce's *Ulysses* (Joyce 1986: 284–313), in which Joyce recasts Nausikaa as Gerty MacDowell, a young woman whose brain has been addled through too much exposure to romances – and who can think of nothing but marriage when she sees the hero, Leopold Bloom. Ask the class to think about the way in which Joyce responds to the Homeric original: how his novel differs in tone and style from Homer's epic; whether Joyce's reworking of the episode implies reverence or antipathy towards the original; what Gerty MacDowell's behaviour tells us about Joyce's view of Nausikaa. Stephen Minta's helpful essay in Graziosi and Greenwood (2007) looks specifically at Joyce's rewriting of the Nausikaa episode.

The class might also consider Book VI in the light of Samuel Butler's theory that the *Odyssey* was written by a Sicilian princess, who represented herself in the poem as Nausikaa (Butler 1897: 200–1).

> She seems to have moved in the best society of her age and country, for we can imagine none more polished on the West coast of Sicily in Odyssean times than the one with which the writer shows herself familiar. She must have had leisure, or she could not have carried through so great a work. She puts up with men when they are necessary or illustrious, but she is never enthusiastic about them, and likes them best when she is laughing at them; but she is cordially interested in fair and famous women.
>
> [...]
>
> Lastly, she must be looked for in one to whom the girl described as Nausicaa was all in all. No one else is drawn with like livingness and enthusiasm, and no other episode is written with the same, or nearly the same, buoyancy of spirits and resiliency of pulse and movement, or brings the scene before us with anything approaching the same freshness, as that in which Nausicaa takes the family linen to, the washing cisterns. The whole of Book VI can only have been written by one who was throwing herself into it heart and soul.

Ask students to pick three moments in Book VI which lend weight to Butler's theory. They might also consider in what way Butler's attitude to the story of Nausikaa differs from Joyce's.

TEACHING BOOK IX

Ask students to consider these questions in advance of the seminar

- How does the shift from third-person to first-person narration affect the way we interpret the narrative in this book (and in Books IX–XII generally)? How does Odysseus tailor the narrative to fit his Phaiakian audience?
- What justifications does Odysseus give for his behaviour towards Polyphemos? How credible are these justifications?
- How is the land of the Cyclopes described? How does its landscape compare to Ithaka, on the one hand, and Phaiakia, on the other?

Seminar activities
Naming. Twice in Book IX – at the Phaiakian banquet (lines 19–28) and in the story of the Cyclops (lines 500–5) – Odysseus reveals his name after a long delay. Ask students to compare his behaviour in these two instances. Why does he conceal his name for so long in each case? What effect does it have when he reveals it?
Colonialism and the Cyclops. Divide students into two groups. Ask one half of the class to explain and defend Odysseus' actions in Book IX. The other half should put the opposite case, explaining – with close reference to the text – how Polyphemos' actions are justified, and how Homer evokes our sympathy for him.

Comparative work: the hero as narrator
Odysseus' narrative is directly imitated in Virgil's *Aeneid*, in which the Trojan hero, Aeneas, gives an account of his wanderings at a banquet in a strange land (in his case Carthage). Close comparison is invited by the fact that the two warriors are supposedly traveling around the Mediterranean at the same time, narrowly missing one another. Ask students to read the following extracts from the *Aeneid*. The first is taken from the start of Aeneas' speech, while in the second he recounts his rescue of Achemenides, a Greek abandoned by Odysseus in Polyphemos' cave. Students should consider: how Aeneas' narrative differs from Odysseus' in terms of style and tone; in what ways Virgil is echoing or imitating Homer, and in what ways he is departing from his example; how Virgil engages with the tales told by Odysseus at the Phaiakian court.

All fell silent now, and their faces were all attention
When from his place of honour Aeneas began to speak: –
 O queen, the griefs you bid me reopen are inexpressible –
The tale of Troy, a rich and most tragic empire
Erased by the Greeks; most piteous events I saw with my own eyes
And played no minor part in. What Myrmidon or Thessalian,
What soldier of fell Ulysses could talk about such events
And keep from tears? Besides, the dewy night drops fast
From heaven, and the declining stars invite to sleep.
But if you want so much to know what happened to us
And hear in brief a recital of Troy's last agony,
Although the memory makes me shudder, and shrink from its
  sadness,
I will attempt it. (*Aeneid* II.1–13, trans. C. Day Lewis (1954))

Towards the well-known shore, mammoth in bulk, his sheep flock
Round him, we saw that same shepherd, that Polyphemus –
A monster, grisly, misshapen, titanic, his eye gone.
He carries the trunk of a pine tree to guide and support him
  walking:
The fleecy sheep go with him – they are his only pleasure
And consolation in woe.
When he had come to the sea's edge and touched the surging deep,
He washed the socket of his eye, which oozed blood, with sea-water,
Gritting his teeth and groaning; then waded into the deep sea,
Yet even there the water did not come up to his waist.
Frightened, we hurried to get far away, taking on board
That Greek who so merited mercy, and stealthily cutting the cables:
Frantically we tugged at the oars, we swept the sea's face.
He sensed us, veered his steps towards the noise of our passage.
But when he found there was no way of laying his hands upon us
And he was falling behind in his race with the waves which carried
  us,
Then he let out a stupendous bellow, shivering the whole
Expanse of the sea, shaking Italy to its core
With fright, and reverberating through Aetna's anfractuous caves.
  (*Aeneid* III.655–74, trans. C. Day Lewis (1954))

TEACHING BOOK XIII

Ask students to consider these questions in advance of the seminar

- Why are the Phaiakians punished? Do we ever find out precisely what happens to them? Does divine justice operate in an intelligible or consistent way in the *Odyssey*? (See Segal 1962 and 1967)

- What is the source of the affinity between Odysseus and Athene? How does it manifest itself over the course of this book?

Seminar activity

Odysseus' lies. Ask students to read closely lines 256–86, the first of Odysseus' lying tales, and to consider both why Odysseus lies at this point, and whether the invented story he tells contains any underlying truths. There are further lying tales at XIV.192–359 (to Eumaios), XVII.415–44 (to Antinoös), XIX.165–299 (to Penelope), and XXIV.244–314 (to Laertes). Divide the students into groups and ask each group to look at one tale: how each invented story relates to Odysseus' own situation; and what elements the various tales have in common.

Comparative work: translations

Athene's speech to Odysseus, in which she reveals herself and exposes his false identity, is a striking one (291–304). The goddess praises Odysseus for qualities which we might not ordinarily regard as heroic. Different translators have approached this potential awkwardness in different ways, and this makes it a good test case for a comparison of translations (though in fact this is a useful exercise with almost any passage – an excellent way of alerting students to the pitfalls of translation, and of words generally). Below are three translations, by Pope (1725–6), Cowper (1791), and Fitzgerald (1961); Lattimore's own version can also be used. Ask students to compare the passages, and to consider: how Athene's tone differs in the four translations; the impression that we get in each translation of Odysseus' character and of the relationship between goddess and hero.

> O still the same *Ulysses*! she rejoin'd,
> In useful craft successfully refin'd!
> Artful in speech, in action, and in mind!
> Suffic'd it not, that thy long labours past
> Secure thou seest thy native shore at last?
> But this to me? who, like thy self, excell
> In arts of counsel, and dissembling well.
> To me, whose wit exceeds the pow'rs divine,
> No less than mortals are surpass'd by thine.
> Know'st not thou me? who made thy life my care,
> Thro' ten years wandering, and thro' ten years war;
> Who taught thee arts, *Alcinous* to persuade,
> To raise his wonder, and engage his aid:
> And now appear, thy treasures to protect,

Conceal thy person, thy designs direct,
And tell thee what thou must from fate expect. (Pope)

Who passes thee in artifice well-fram'd
And in imposture various, need shall find
Of all his policy, although a God.
Canst thou not cease, inventive as thou art
And subtle, from the wiles which thou hast lov'd
Since thou wast infant, and from tricks of speech
Delusive, even in thy native land?
But come, dismiss we these ingenious shifts
From our discourse, in which we both excel;
For thou of all men in expedients most
Abound'st and eloquence, and I, throughout
All heav'n have praise for wisdom and for art.
And know'st thou not thine Athenæan aid,
Pallas, Jove's daughter, who in all thy toils
Assist thee and defend? I gave thee pow'r
T' engage the hearts of all Phæacia's sons,
And here arrive ev'n now, counsels to frame
Discrete with thee, and to conceal the stores
Giv'n to thee by the rich Phæacian Chiefs
On my suggestion, at thy going thence. (Cowper)

Whoever gets around you must be sharp
and guileful as a snake; even a god
might bow to you in ways of dissimulation.
You! You chameleon!
Bottomless bag of tricks! Here in your own country
would you not give your stratagems a rest
or stop spellbinding for an instant?

You play your part as if it were your own tough skin.

No more of this, though. Two of a kind, we are,
contrivers, both. Of all men now alive
you are the best in plots and story-telling.
My own fame is for wisdom among the gods –
deceptions, too.
                              Would even you have guessed
that I am Pallas Athene, daughter of Zeus,
I that am always with you in times of trial,
a shield to you in battle, I who made
the Phaiakians befriend you, to a man?
Now I am here again to counsel with you – (Fitzgerald)

TEACHING BOOK XXIII

Ask students to consider these questions in advance of the seminar

- At what point does Penelope recognise Odysseus? It may be helpful to look at XIX.100–599, when he speaks to her while still disguised as a beggar.
- What similarities are there between Odysseus and Penelope? How (if at all) are they shown to be well-matched?
- Is there anything in Odysseus' final appearance in his household which suggests that he has developed – morally or intellectually – over the course of his wanderings?

Seminar activities
Penelope's Trick. Ask students to read closely lines 173–204, and consider: why Penelope tricks Odysseus in this way; what this tells us about their relationship; whether their bed has a larger significance. (They should also look at Telemachos' speech at XVI.31–5, where the bed is first mentioned.)
Ending the *Odyssey*. The critic Aristarchos thought the poem originally ended at line 296 (when Odysseus and Penelope go to bed) – a judgement shared by some modern critics. Divide the class into two groups, and ask one group to make the case for ending the poem at this moment, while the other one argues for the ending as we currently have it.

Comparative work: Atwood's Penelope
Margaret Atwood's *Penelopiad* (2005) tells the story of the *Odyssey* from Penelope's perspective. This is a brief extract from her account of the events of Book XXIII:

> The hardness of my heart was a notion I was glad to foster, however, as it would reassure Odysseus to know that I hadn't been throwing myself into the arms of every man who'd turned up claiming to be him. So I looked at him blankly, and said it was too much for me to swallow, the idea that this dirty, blood-stained vagabond was the same as my fine husband who had sailed away, so beautifully dressed, twenty years before.
>
> Odysseus grinned – he was looking forward to the big revelation scene, the part where I would say, 'It was you all along! What a terrific disguise!' and throw my arms around his neck. Then he went off to take a much-needed bath. When he came back in clean clothes, smelling a good deal better than when he'd gone, I couldn't resist teasing him one last time. I ordered Eurycleia to move the bed outside the bedroom of Odysseus, and to make it up for the stranger.

You'll recall that one post of this bed was carved from a tree still rooted in the ground. Nobody knew about it except Odysseus, myself, and my maid Actoris, from Sparta, who by that time was long dead.

Assuming that someone had cut through his cherished bedpost, Odysseus lost his temper at once. Only then did I relent, and go through the business of recognising him. I shed a satisfactory number of tears, and embraced him, and claimed that he'd passed the bedpost test, and that I was now convinced. (169–71)

Ask students to consider whether this passage is compatible with a close reading of Book XXIII, picking out passages which either support or weaken Atwood's view of Penelope.

Chapter 6

Suggested Further Reading

This is not intended to be an exhaustive account of relevant scholarship. More has been written on Homer than on any other poet (possibly excepting Shakespeare), and exhaustiveness is not possible, or desirable. I have tried to focus on works which do not assume knowledge of Greek.

General Works on Epic

Beye (1968) is an approachable starting point. There are also good general studies by Toohey (1992) and King (2009).

On Oral Poetry and the Homeric Question

Hainsworth, *The Idea of Epic* (1991: 1–45) provides a good, very basic overview of the topic. Fowler's own essay in Fowler (2005) offers a rather more sophisticated one. The starting point for any detailed investigation must be Parry (1971), though his work can be technical, and assumes knowledge of Greek. His ideas are further developed in Lord (1960) and Foley (1991). Janko (1998) offers a clear and sane account of the theory that the Homeric poems were oral works, dictated to a scribe. Powell (1991) argues that the Greek alphabet originated in order that the Homeric poems might be transcribed. Nagy (see, for example, 1996) has published prolifically on his 'evolutionary' account of Homeric verse. Recent studies have increasingly focused on the role of the audience in the creation of oral poetry: Bakker and Kahane (1997) draw together several excellent essays concerned with this approach; see also Scodel (2002). For those who want to go back to the origins of the modern debate, Wolf's 1795 work has been translated into English (Wolf 1985).

General works on Homer

Kirk (1962) still provides a good starting point, focusing on the social, historical, and linguistic background to the poems. Some excellent introductory works have also been published in the past thirty years. Griffin (1980a) is a very slim but sensitive introduction. Rutherford (1996) is more detailed, and does an excellent job of synthesising recent scholarship. Powell (2004) is excellent and very readable, though the author is keen to press his own highly contentious solution to the Homeric question. Griffin (1980b) is one of the very best – and most approachable – general works on Homer, making a strong case for reading the poems as poems (rather than regarding them as scraps of archaeological evidence). Fowler (2005) brings together some very good essays, mostly on aspects of the poem's interpretation and reception; particularly useful are those by Silk (on the *Odyssey*), Scodel (on the relationship between the oral poet and his audience), by Buxton (on similes), and by Fowler himself. Equally useful, but with more of an emphasis on the origins and context of the poems are the essays in Morris and Powell (1997). The German essays translated by Jones and Wright (1997) are also worth reading.

On the *Iliad*

Silk (2004) gives an excellent – and occasionally contentious – introduction. Taplin (1992) offers a persuasive account of how the poem might originally have been performed, looking closely at its structure as well as its poetry – his work also has implications for the way we read the *Odyssey*. Schein (1984) looks at the poem's grand themes: war, death, and glory. See also the essays collected by Cairns (2001). Pucci (1987) discusses connections between the *Iliad* and the *Odyssey*.

On the *Odyssey*

There is a good commentary by Heubeck, West and Hainsworth (1988–92), though it sometimes suffers from the divergent viewpoints of its various contributors. Jones (1988) provides a thorough, lively, and intelligent commentary for the Greekless reader, basing it on Lattimore's translation. There is a commentary on Books VI–VII only by Garvie (1994). Jong (2001) is a narratalogical commentary, which does an excellent job of drawing out the poem's elaborate structure, echoes and foreshadowings. Griffin (2004) is an enjoyable, brief introduction to the poem. Schein (1996) and Doherty (2009) are both collections of important – and generally accessible – essays.

Clay (1983) looks at the role of the gods in the poem, and their relationship to mankind (on which see also Marks 2008). A good deal of recent criticism has focused on the role and representation of women in the poem – and especially on the figure of Penelope; see in particular, Katz (1991), Felson-Rubin (1994), and Doherty (1990). Murnaghan (1987) looks at the prevalence of lying, disguise and recognition in the poem. On Odysseus' deceptions, see also Walcot (2009). Richardson (2006) examines narrative deceptions by the poet himself. Rose (1975) and Thalmann (1998) look at the way in which social class in represented in the Odyssey. Malkin (1998) is concerned with issues of race and colonialism.

On Book I, Clay (1976) and Walsh (1995) both give a useful discussion of the poem's opening, while Olson (1990) looks at the recurring story of Agamemnon's disastrous return, which plays such a prominent role. On Telemachos' role, see Alden (1987). On Book VI, see Cairns (1990) on the threat to Nausikaa's reputation; Shapiro (1995) stresses the eroticism of the encounter. On Book IX, O'Sullivan (1990) looks at the representation of nature and culture in the Polyphemos episode, while Austin (1983) offers a particularly challenging account of Odysseus' relationship with the Cyclops. On Book XIII, Segal (1962 and 1967) looks at the ritual significance of Odysseus' return, and at the role played by the gods. Much of the gender-focused criticism mentioned above concerns itself particularly with Book XXIII; see also Fredericksmeyer (1997) on Penelope's trickery and Emlyn-Jones (2009) on the reunion between Odysseus and Penelope.

On the Reception of the *Odyssey*

Hall (2008) is an outstandingly readable and suggestive account of the poem's rich reception history – particularly good on film and recent fiction. Stanford (1954), which focuses on the figure of Odysseus, is still useful. Many of the essays in Fowler (2005) deal with the poem's reception, notably those by Wilson (on English epic), Steiner (on Homer in translation) and Zajko (on *Ulysses*). Graziosi and Greenwood (2007) is a collection of essays on recent interpretations of Homer; the chapters by Haubold (on the way Milman Parry's research has affected Homer's reception), Minta (on Joyce's reworking of the Nausikaa episode) and Goldhill (on cinematic reworkings) are particularly useful for students of the *Odyssey*. Burrow (1993) traces a line of descent from Homer to Milton, via various other epic poets. Steiner (1996) is a collection of excerpts from various translations of Homer. Also worth consulting are in-depth studies of the translations by Chapman (Lord 1956) and Pope (Sowerby 1995). For an overview of Homeric translation see Underwood (1998). For a study of Kazantzakis' debt to Homer see Levitt (1983). On Derek Walcott see Taplin (1991).

Online Resources

There are two websites of particular value to students of the *Odyssey*. The first is the Chicago Homer site, edited by Ahuvia Kahane and Martin Mueller, which offers a fully searchable text of both of the Homeric poems (and several other works) in Greek, English, and German. Users can click on any Greek word to see a list of its other appearance in the text. They can also click for a translation of any word <http://digital.library.northwestern.edu/homer/>.

   The Perseus Project at Tufts University gives access to a vast range of Greek and Latin texts, both in original and in translation <http://www.perseus.tufts.edu/hopper/>.

References

Adorno, Theodor, and Max Horkheimer [1944] (2002), *Dialectic of Enlightenment: Philosophical Fragments*, ed. by Gunzelin Schmid Noerr, trans. Edmund Jephcott, Stanford: Stanford University Press.

Alden, M. J. (1987), 'The role of Telemachus in the *Odyssey*', *Hermes* 115: 129–37.

Amory, A. (1963), 'The reunion of Odysseus and Penelope', in *Essays on the Odyssey*, ed. C. H. Taylor, Jr., Bloomington: Indiana University Press, pp. 100–21.

Arnold, Matthew (1960), *The Complete Prose Works of Matthew Arnold, Volume I: On the Classical Tradition*, ed. R. H. Super, Ann Arbor: University of Michigan Press.

Atwood, Margaret (2005), *The Penelopiad*, Edinburgh: Canongate.

Austin, Norman (1975), *Archery at the Dark of the Moon: Poetic Problems in Homer's Odyssey*, Berkeley: University of California Press.

Austin, Norman (1983), 'Odysseus and the Cyclops: Who is who?', in *Approaches to Homer*, ed. C. A. Rubino and C. W. Shelmerdine, Austin: University of Texas Press, pp. 3–37.

Bakker, Egbert, and Ahuvia Kahane (eds) (1997), *Written Voices, Spoken Signs: Tradition, Performance, and the Epic Text*, Cambridge, MA: Harvard University Press.

Beasley, Jerry C. (1982), *Novels of the 1740s*, Athens, GA: University of Georgia Press.

Bergren, Ann L. T. (1981), 'Helen's "Good Drug": *Odyssey* IV 1–305', in *Contemporary Literary Hermeneutics and Interpretation of Classical Texts*, ed. Stephanus Kresic, Ottawa: University of Ottawa Press, pp. 201–14.

Beye, Charles Rowan (1968), *The Iliad, the Odyssey, and the Epic Tradition*, London: Macmillan.

Bittlestone, Robert, with James Diggle and John Underhill (2005), *Odysseus Unbound: The Search for Homer's Ithaca*, Cambridge: Cambridge University Press.

Borris, Kenneth (2000), *Allegory and Epic in English Renaissance Literature:*

Heroic Form in Sidney, Spenser, and Milton, Cambridge: Cambridge University Press.

Bradford, Ernle (1963), *Ulysses Found*, London: Hodder and Stoughton.

Burrow, Colin (1993), *Epic Romance: Homer to Milton*, Oxford: Oxford University Press.

Butcher, S. H., and A. Lang (1879), *The Odyssey of Homer, Done into English Prose* Macmillan: London.

Butler, Samuel (1897), *The Authoress of the Odyssey*, London: Longman.

Butler, Samuel (1900), *The Odyssey: Rendered into English Prose for the Use of Those who Cannot Read the Original*, London: A. C. Fitfield.

Butler, Samuel (1917), *The Note-Books of Samuel Butler*, ed. Henry Festing Jones, London: Jonathan Cape.

Butler, Samuel (1934), *Further Extracts from the Note-Books of Samuel Butler*, ed. Henry Festing Jones, London: Jonathan Cape.

Cairns, Douglas L. (1990), 'Mixing with men and Nausicaa's nemesis', *Classical Quarterly* 40: 263–6.

Cairns, Douglas L. (ed.) (2001), *Oxford Readings in Homer's Iliad*, Oxford: Oxford University Press.

Chapman, George (2000), *Chapman's Homer: The Odyssey*, ed. Allardyce Nicoll, Princeton: Princeton University Press.

Clay, Jenny Strauss (1976), 'The beginning of the Odyssey', *American Journal of Philology* 97: 313–26.

Clay, Jenny Strauss (1983), *The Wrath of Athena: Gods and Men in the Odyssey*, Princeton: Princeton University Press.

Cook, Erwin F. (1995), *The Odyssey in Athens: Myths of Cultural Origins*, Ithaca, NY: Cornell University Press.

Cowper, William (1809), *The Odyssey of Homer, Translated into Blank Verse*, 3rd edn, London: J. Johnson.

Davidson, James (1997), 'Like a meteorite', *London Review of Books* 19.15: 3–6.

Day Lewis, C. (trans.) (1954), *The Aeneid of Virgil*, London: Hogarth Press.

Doherty, Lilian E. (1990), *Siren Songs: Gender, Audience, and Narrators in the Odyssey*, Oxford: Oxford University Press.

Doherty, Lilian E. (ed.) (2009), *Homer's Odyssey*, Oxford Readings in Classical Studies, Oxford: Oxford University Press.

Ellman, Richard (1959), *James Joyce*, Oxford: Oxford University Press.

Emlyn-Jones, Chris (2009), 'The reunion of Penelope and Odysseus', in Lilian E. Doherty (ed.), *Homer's Odyssey*, Oxford Readings in Classical Studies, Oxford: Oxford University Press, pp. 208–330.

Farron, S. G. (1979–80), 'The *Odyssey* as an anti-aristocratic statement', *Studies in Antiquity* 1: 59–101.

Faulkner, Peter (1973), *William Morris: The Critical Heritage*, London: Routledge.

Felson-Rubin, Nancy (1994), *Regarding Penelope: From Character to Poetics*, Princeton: Princeton University Press.

Fénelon, Francois de (1994), *Telemachus, Son of Ulysses,* ed. Patrick Riley, Cambridge: Cambridge University Press.

Fielding, Henry [1749] (2005), *The History of Tom Jones, A Foundling*, ed. Thomas Keymer and Alice Wakeley, Harmondsworth: Penguin.

Fitzgerald, Robert (1961), *Homer's The Odyssey*, New York: Farrar, Straus and Giroux.

Foley, John Miles (1991), *Immanent Art: From Structure to Meaning in Traditional Oral Epic*, Bloomington: Indiana University Press.

Fowler, Robert (ed.) (2005), *The Cambridge Companion to Homer*, Cambridge: Cambridge University Press.

Fredericksmeyer, H. C. (1997), 'Penelope *polutropos*: *Odyssey* 23. 218–24', *American Journal of Philology* 118: 487–97.

Garvie, A. F. (1994), *Homer: Odyssey, Books VI–VII*, Cambridge: Cambridge University Press.

Goldhill, Simon (1991), *The Poet's Voice: Essays on Poetics and Greek Literature*, Cambridge: Cambridge University Press.

Goldhill, Simon (2007), '*Naked* and O *Brother, Where Art Thou?*: The Politics and Poetics of Epic Cinema', in Barbara Graziosi and Emily Greenwood (eds), *Homer in the Twentieth Century: Between World Literature and the Western Canon*, Oxford: Oxford University Press, pp. 245–67.

Gould, J. (1973), 'Hiketeia', *Journal of Hellenic Studies* 93: 74–103.

Graves, Robert (1960), *The Greek Myths*, 2 vols, 2nd edn, Harmondsworth: Penguin.

Graziosi, Barbara, and Emily Greenwood (eds) (2007), *Homer in the Twentieth Century: Between World Literature and the Western Canon*, Oxford: Oxford University Press.

Griffin, Jasper (1980a), *Homer*, Oxford: Oxford University Press.

Griffin, Jasper (1980b), *Homer on Life and Death*, Oxford: Oxford University Press.

Griffin, Jasper (2004), *Homer: The Odyssey*, 2nd edn, Cambridge: Cambridge University Press.

Hainsworth, J. B. (1991), *The Idea of Epic*, Berkeley and Los Angeles: University of California Press.

Hall, Edith (2008), *The Return of Ulysses: A Cultural History of Homer's Odyssey*, London: I. B. Tauris.

Hare, Steve (2008), 'A history of Penguin Classics', in Russell Edwards, Steve Hare and Jim Robinson (eds), *Penguin Classics*, Penguin Collectors Society, pp. 24–32.

Harrison, S. J. (1990), 'Some Odyssean scenes in Apuleius' *Metamorphoses*', *MD* 25: 193–201.

Haubold, Johannes (2007), 'Homer after Parry: Tradition, reception, and the timeless text', in Barbara Graziosi and Emily Greenwood (eds), *Homer in the Twentieth Century: Between World Literature and the Western Canon*, Oxford: Oxford University Press, pp. 27–46.

Heath, Michael (2000), 'Do heroes eat fish?', in David Braund and John Wilkins (eds), *Athenaeus and His World: Reading Greek Culture in the Roman Empire*, Exeter: University of Exeter Press, pp. 342–52.

Heliodorus (1957), *An Ethiopian Romance*, trans. Moses Hadas, Ann Arbor: University of Michigan Press.

Hesiod (1964), *The Works and Days, Theogony, The Shield of Herakles*, trans. Richmond Lattimore, Ann Arbor: University of Michigan.

Heubeck, Alfred, and Arie Hoekstra (1989), *A Commentary on Homer's Odyssey, Volume 2: Books IX–XVI*, Oxford: Clarendon Press.

Heubeck, Alfred, Joseph Russo and Manuel Fernandez-Galiano (1992), *A Commentary on Homer's Odyssey, Volume 3: Books XVII–XXIV*, Oxford: Clarendon Press.

Heubeck, Alfred, Stephanie West and J. B. Hainsworth (1988), *A Commentary on Homer's Odyssey, Volume 1: Books I–VIII*, Oxford: Clarendon Press.

Hobbes, Thomas (2008), *Translations of Homer: The Iliad and the Odyssey*, ed. Eric Nelson, 2 vols, Oxford: Oxford University Press.

Hurst, Isobel (2006), *Victorian Women Writers and the Classics: The Feminine of Homer*, Oxford: Oxford University Press.

Janko, R. (1982), *Homer, Hesiod and the Hymns: Diachronic Development in Epic Diction*, Cambridge: Cambridge University Press.

Janko, R. (1998), 'The Homeric poems as oral dictated texts', *Classical Quarterly* 48: 1–13.

Jenkyns, Richard (1980), *The Victorians and Ancient Greece*, Oxford: Blackwell.

Jones, P. V., and G. M. Wright (ed. and trans.) (1997), *Homer: German Scholarship in Translation*, Oxford: Clarendon Press.

Jones, Peter (1988), *Homer's Odyssey: A Companion to the English Translation of Richmond Lattimore*, Bristol: Bristol Classical Press.

Jong, Irene de (2001), *A Narratological Commentary on the Odyssey*, Cambridge: Cambridge University Press.

Joyce, James (1986), *Ulysses: The Corrected Text, Student's Edition*, Harmondsworth: Penguin.

Katz, Marilyn A. (1991), *Penelope's Renown: Meaning and Indeterminacy in the Odyssey*, Princeton: Princeton University Press.

Kazantzakis, Nikos [1938] (1958), *The Odyssey: A Modern Sequel*, trans. Kimon Friar, London: Secker and Warburg.

Keats, John (1978), *Complete Poems*, ed. Jack Stillinger, Cambridge, MA: Harvard University Press.

Kenner, Hugh (1972), *The Pound Era*, London: Faber & Faber.

King, Katherine Callen (2009), *Ancient Epic*, Oxford: Blackwell.

Kirk, G. S. (1962), *The Songs of Homer*, Cambridge: Cambridge University Press.

Kirk, G. S. (1976), *Homer and the Oral Tradition*, Cambridge: Cambridge University Press.

Konstan, David, and D. A. Russell (2005), *Heraclitus: Homeric Problems*, Atlanta: Society of Biblical Literature.

Lane Patey, Douglas (1997), 'Ancients and Moderns', in *The Cambridge History of Literary Criticism, Volume IV: The Eighteenth Century*, ed. H. B. Nisbet and Claude Rawson, Cambridge: Cambridge University Press, pp. 32–71

Lattimore, Richmond (trans.) (1951), *The Iliad*, Chicago: University of Chicago Press.

Lattimore, Richmond (trans.) (1965), *The Odyssey of Homer*, New York: Harper.

Lawrence, T. E. (1932), *The Odyssey of Homer*, New York: Oxford University Press.

Levine, Joseph M. (1991), *The Battle of the Books: History and Literature in the Augustan Age*, Ithaca, NY: Cornell University Press.

Levitt, Morton B. (1983), 'Homer, Joyce, Kazantzakis: Modernism and the epic tradition', *Journal of the. Hellenic Diaspora* 10.4: 41–5.

Locke, John (1988), *Two Treatises of Government*, ed. Peter Laslett, Cambridge: Cambridge University Press.

Longinus (1965), *On the Sublime*, ed. and trans. D. A. Russell, Oxford: Oxford University Press.

Lord, Albert B. (1960), *The Singer of Tales*, Cambridge, MA: Harvard University Press.

Lord, George de F. (1956), *Homeric Renaissance: The Odyssey of George Chapman*, New Haven: Yale University Press.

McCarthy, Fiona (1994), *William Morris: A Life for Our Time*, London: Faber & Faber.

Maginn, William (1850), *Homeric Ballads*, London: John W. Parker.

Malkin, Irad (1998), *The Returns of Odysseus: Colonization and Ethnicity*, Berkeley and Los Angeles: University of California Press.

Marks, J. (2008), *Zeus in the Odyssey*, Cambridge, MA: Harvard University Press.

Mason, H. A. (1972), *To Homer through Pope: An Introduction to Homer's Iliad and Pope's Translation*, London: Chatto & Windus.

Milton, John ([1667] 1998), *Paradise Lost*, ed. Alistair Fowler, 2nd edn, London: Longman.

Minta, Stephen (2007), 'Homer and Joyce: The case of Nausicaa', in Barbara Graziosi and Emily Greenwood (eds), *Homer in the Twentieth Century: Between World Literature and the Western Canon*, Oxford: Oxford University Press, pp. 92–119.

Morris, Ian, and Barry Powell (eds) (1997), *A New Companion to Homer*, Brill: Leiden.

Morris, William (1887), *The Odyssey of Homer, done into English verse*, London: Reeves and Turner.

Most, Glen W. (1989), 'The Structure and Function of Odysseus' *Apologoi*', *Transactions of the American Philological Association* 119: 15–30.

Murnaghan, Sheila (1987), *Disguise and Recognition in the Odyssey*, Princeton: Princeton University Press.

Musgrave, William (1865), *The Odyssey of Homer rendered into English blank verse*, London: Bell and Daldy.

Nagy, Geoffrey (1996), *Homeric Questions*, Austin: University of Texas Press.

O'Sullivan, J. N. (1990), 'Nature and culture in Odyssey 9', *Symbolae Osloenses* 65: 7–17.

Ogilby, John (1665), *Homer, his Odysses translated, adorn'd with sculpture, and illustrated with annotations*, London: Thomas Roycroft.

Olson, S. Douglas (1990), 'The stories of Agamemnon in Homer's *Odyssey*', *Transactions of the American Philological Association* 120: 57–72.

Olson, S. Douglas, and Alexander Sens (1999), *Matro of Pitane and the Tradition of Epic Parody in the Fourth Century BCE: Text, Translation, and Commentary*, Atlanta, GA: American Philological Association.

Page, D. L. (1955), *The Homeric Odyssey*, Oxford: Oxford University Press.

Parry, Adam M. (1989), *The Language of Achilles and Other Papers*, ed. P. H. J. Lloyd-Jones, Oxford: Clarendon Press.

Parry, Milman (1971), *The Making of Homeric Verse: The Collected Papers of Milman Parry*, ed. Adam M. Parry, Oxford: Clarendon Press.

Petronius (1997), *The Satyricon*, trans. P. G. Walsh, Oxford: Oxford University Press.

Pope, Alexander (1967), *The Twickenham Edition of the Poems of Alexander Pope, Volumes IX–X: The Odyssey of Homer*, ed. Maynard Mack, London: Methuen.

Pope, Alexander (1993), *Alexander Pope*, ed. Pat Rogers, The Oxford Authors, Oxford: Oxford University Press.

Powell, Barry P. (1991), *Homer and the Origin of the Greek Alphabet*, Cambridge: Cambridge University Press.

Powell, Barry P. (2004), *Homer*, Oxford: Blackwell.

Pucci, Pietro (1987), *Odysseus Polutropos: Intertextual Readings in the Odyssey and the Iliad*, Ithaca, New York: Cornell University Press.

Richardson, Scott (2006), 'The devious narrator of the *Odyssey*', *Classical Journal* 101.4: 337–59.

Rieu, E.V. (1946), *Homer: The Odyssey*, Harmondsworth: Penguin.

Rose, Peter W. (1975), 'Class ambivalence in the *Odyssey*', *Historia* 24: 129–49.

Rutherford, Richard (1996), *Homer*, Oxford: Oxford University Press.

Sandy, Gerald, and Stephen Harrison (2008), 'Novels ancient and modern', in Tim Whitmarsh (ed.), *The Cambridge Companion to the Greek and Roman Novel*, Cambridge: Cambridge University Press, pp. 299–320.

Schein, Seth L. (1984), *The Mortal Hero: An Introduction to Homer's Iliad*, Berkeley and Los Angeles: University of California Press.

Schein, Seth L. (ed.) (1996), *Reading the Odyssey: Selected Interpretive Essays*, Princeton: Princeton University Press.

Scodel, Ruth (2002), *Listening to Homer: Tradition, Narrative, and Audience*, Ann Arbor: University of Michigan Press.

Seaford, Richard (1994), *Reciprocity and Ritual: Homer and Tragedy in the Developing City-State*, Oxford: Clarendon Press.

Segal, Charles (1962), 'The Phaeacians and the symbolism of Odysseus' Return', *Arion* 1.4: 17–64.

Segal, Charles (1967), 'Transition and ritual in Odysseus' Return', *Parola del Passato* 22: 332–42.

Shapiro, Harold A. (1995), 'Coming of age in Phaiakia: The Meeting of Odysseus and Nausikaa', in Beth Cohen (ed.), *The Distaff Side: Representing the Female in Homer's Odyssey*, Oxford: Oxford University Press, pp. 155–64.

Sherratt, E. S. (1990), '"Reading the Texts": Archaeology and the Homeric question', *Antiquity* 64: 807–24.

Silk, Michael (2004) *Homer: The Iliad*, 2nd edn, Cambridge: Cambridge University Press.

Sowerby, Robin (1995), 'The Augustan *Odyssey*', *Translation and Literature* 4: 157–82

Stanford, W. B. (1954), *The Ulysses Theme: A Study in the Adaptability of a Traditional Hero*, Oxford: Blackwell.

Steiner, George (1996), *Homer in English*, Harmondsworth: Penguin.

Steiner, George (2005), 'Homer in English translation', in Robert Fowler (ed.), *The Cambridge Companion to Homer*, Cambridge: Cambridge University Press, pp. 363–75.

Taplin, Oliver (1991), 'Derek Walcott's *Omeros* and Derek Walcott's Homer', *Arion* 3rd series, 1.2: 213–26.

Taplin, Oliver (1992), *Homeric Soundings: The Shaping of the Iliad*, Oxford: Clarendon Press.

Thalmann, William G. (1998), *The Swineherd and the Bow: Representations of Class in the Odyssey*, Ithaca, NY: Cornell University Press.

Toohey, Peter (1992), *Reading Epic: An Introduction to the Ancient Narratives*, London: Routledge.

Underwood, Simeon (1998), *English Translators of Homer: From George Chapman to Christopher Logue*, Plymouth: Northcote House.

Vidal-Naquet, Pierre (1996), 'Land and sacrifice in the *Odyssey*: A study of religious and mythical meanings', in Seth L. Schein (ed.), *Reading the*

Odyssey: Selected Interpretive Essays, Princeton: Princeton University Press, pp. 33–53.

Voltaire (1727), *Essay on Epick Poetry*, London: for S. Jallason.

Walcott, Derek (1990), *Omeros*, London: Faber & Faber.

Walcot, Peter (2009), 'Odysseus and the art of lying', in Lilian E. Doherty, *Homer's Odyssey*, Oxford Readings in Classical Studies, Oxford: Oxford University Press, pp. 135–54.

Walsh, T. R. (1995), '*Odyssey* I.6–9: A little more than kine', *Mnemosyne* 48: 385–410.

West, M. L. (1988), 'The rise of the Greek epic', *Journal of Hellenic Studies* 108: 151–72.

Wilson, Penelope (2005), 'Homer and English epic', in Robert Fowler (ed.), *The Cambridge Companion to Homer*, Cambridge: Cambridge University Press, pp. 278–86.

Winkler, John J. (1990), *The Constraints of Desire: The Anthropology of Sex and Gender in Ancient Greece*, London: Routledge.

Wolf, F. A. (1985), *Prolegomena to Homer*, trans. A. Grafton, G. W. Most and J. E. G. Zetzel, Princeton: Princeton University Press.

Worsley, P. S. (1861–2), *The Odyssey of Homer, translated into English verse in the Spenserian stanza*, 2 vols, Edinburgh: William Blackwood.

Wynter, Sylvia (2002), '"A different kind of creature": Caribbean literature, the Cyclops factor and the second poetics of the propter nos', in Timothy J. Reiss (ed.), *Sisyphus and Eldorado: Magical and Other Realisms in Caribbean Literature*, Trenton, NJ: African World Press, 2002, pp. 143–67.

Zajko, Vanda (2005), 'Homer and *Ulysses*', in Robert Fowler (ed.), *The Cambridge Companion to Homer*, Cambridge: Cambridge University Press, pp. 311–23.

Index